Ali in Wonderland

"Hilarious." —*Marie Claire*

"She's funny and engaging, warm and intelligent. She's the girlfriend you want to have a glass of wine with, the one who makes you laugh because she sees the funny and the absurd in everything. So, yes, reminiscent of a certain Oscar speech, I like her. I really like her! But more than that, I like her book." —*Huffington Post*

"Ali Wentworth's book is like *Chicken Soup for the Vagina*. Gays and straight men, I'm not leaving you out here! Ali is truly one of the quickest, funniest girls I've ever met. Enjoy!" —Kathy Griffin

"A satirical dissection of class and privilege. . . . A smart, often-funny memoir." —*Kirkus Reviews*

"Unanimous applause greeted this actress-comedian's tour of her fabulous life . . . all recounted in a manner that had one reader wondering if Wentworth is 'a long-lost sister of the Sedaris clan.'" —*Elle* (Readers' Prize)

"One of the most hilarious reads I've enjoyed in a long time." —Gwyneth Paltrow

"Wentworth is amusing and frank, often frenetic, with sharp intelligence underneath the sassy wackiness; passages about her struggle with depression, falling in love with her husband, and her daughter's baptism have funny moments, but they're thoughtful and touching, too. . . . Highly entertaining." —*Publishers Weekly*

"Ali Wentworth tumbles comically through *Ali in Wonderland*." —*Vanity Fair*

"Everything that comes out of Ali Wentworth's mouth is funny!" —Jerry Seinfeld

"A breezily amusing memoir." —*New York Post*

"Ali Wentworth is funny and warm and crazy all at once. Like Barbara Eden. But on something. Like crystal meth." —Alec Baldwin

"With candor and humor, [Wentworth] writes about her life, her marriage, and growing up in the elite world of her illustrious mother." —Julie Hinds, *Detroit Free Press*

"Ali has written a truly hilarious book . . . and she's also a good kisser!" —Chelsea Handler

"I would tone down the pee and fart references." —Muffie Cabot (Ali's mother)

ali in

WONDERLAND

ali in WONDERLAND

and other tall tales

ALI WENTWORTH

HARPER

NEW YORK · LONDON · TORONTO · SYDNEY

HARPER

A hardcover edition of this book was published in 2012 by HarperCollins Publishers.

"The Eyes Have It," the final chapter of this edition, was originally published in the January 2013 edition of *Elle*.

HarperCollins books may be purchased for educational, business, or sales promotional use. For information please write: Special Markets Department, HarperCollins Publishers, 10 East 53rd Street, New York, NY 10022.

FIRST HARPER PAPERBACK PUBLISHED 2013.

Designed by William Ruoto

Library of Congress Cataloging-in-Publication Data is available upon request.

ISBN 978-0-06-199858-4 (pbk.)

13 14 15 16 17 OV/RRD 10 9 8 7 6 5 4 3

THE NAMES AND FACES IN THIS BOOK HAVE BEEN

CHANGED TO PROTECT MY INNOCENCE.

To my mother for what she taught me . . .

*To my daughters for forgiving me what
I taught them.*

"Well-behaved women seldom make history."

—A BUMPER STICKER

contents

CHAPTER 1

Nobody Goes to the Bahamas in July   1

CHAPTER 2

Mama, Can You Hear Me?   15

CHAPTER 3

Just a Spoon Full of Something   23

CHAPTER 4

Don't Look Back   35

CHAPTER 5

Girls, Interrupted   45

CHAPTER 6

Hugs Not Drugs   57

CHAPTER 7

Mi Familia!   71

contents

CHAPTER 8
Happy and Preppy
and Bursting with Love 81

CHAPTER 9
Tennis, Anyone? 93

CHAPTER 10
London Calling 99

CHAPTER 11
What Color Is My Parachute? 107

CHAPTER 12
The Four Seasons 115

CHAPTER 13
Ali in Wonderland 125

CHAPTER 14
French Kiss-Off 133

CHAPTER 15
Elevator Down 149

CHAPTER 16
Home Box Office 157

CHAPTER 17
Like a Good Melon, You Know 171

contents

CHAPTER 18

Tied in Knots 179

CHAPTER 19

There's No Uterus Like My Uterus 189

CHAPTER 20

Well-Mannered 197

CHAPTER 21

Coming Home 205

CHAPTER 22

A Big Bowl of Baby 211

CHAPTER 23

I Don't Get Vacation 217

CHAPTER 24

Ali Sells Seashells 229

CHAPTER 25

I Was Born This Way 239

CHAPTER 26

The Eyes Have It 245

Acknowledgments 253

About the Author 255

nobody goes to the bahamas in july

There is a moment in every woman's life in which she becomes completely unzipped, demented, whacked, non compos mentis—for some it lasts minutes; for others, their entire lives. I have exemplary friends; many are CEOs of corporations or volunteers for nonprofits, almost all are meritorious mothers and ethical women. But if you gave them each a glass of pinot noir and a cushy ottoman, they would regale you with stories of the time they went bonkers.

I cracked like a Baccarat tumbler on a slate floor in Santa Monica, California, fourteen years ago. I was living at the time with a towering Jewish comedy writer named Ari. I was in awe of his deranged outlook on life and shock-jock sense of humor. He was brilliant, cynical, and wildly funny; I never tired of his monologues on everything from Britney Spears to Nazi Germany. I met him in Los Angeles, but like me, he was from the East Coast and knew what real snow looked like, as opposed to the tons of soap flakes Aaron Spelling had trucked in for his holiday party. There was a familiarity about Ari; it was as if we'd known each other since Hebrew school (as a Protestant I've never been, but you get the gist). There's a scene in the movie *Broadcast News* when Albert Brooks says to Holly Hunter, "I'll meet you at the place, near the thing, where we went that time"—that was our constant dialogue. We were ultimately better suited as naughty siblings than mates and preferred ridiculing celebrity sex tapes to making our own. We bought a house in L.A. that became a fortress against all the hardships of the Hollywood grind.

Ari spent most of his time writing and decorating the house with Moroccan antiques and twelve-foot Persian rugs. We swam in our black-bottomed granite pool and threw infamous Christmas parties. (Not at the same time.) There was always an abundance of liquor, glazed hams, spinach dip, hummus, gingerbread cookies, and a giant Christmas tree, which Ari, being Jewish, always protested against. The party would be sprinkled with just enough celebrity to be titillating: Michael Keaton, Sandra Bernhardt, and once, the gorgeous Robin Wright. All brought by other people. For us, getting the guy who did our taxes to come was a triumph.

We would drive to San Francisco just to eat at a hole-in-the-wall Chinese restaurant with soup dumplings that melt in your mouth. We hiked canyons with our dogs, had brunch with people who were also running like frenzied rodents in the Hollywood Habitrail, and hit every Sunday-morning flea market from Orange County to Long Beach. We were slowly scaling the wall of middling success; he was churning out TV pilots and I was auditioning for everything from the cop dramas in which I would only scream, "Get down! He has a gun!" to Lifetime movies about runaway pregnant teens. Occasionally I would read for the pretty blond lead, but I would invariably receive uplifting feedback like, "She's a seven, we need a ten!" Ari bought a tiny apartment in Manhattan so we could have a safety raft when Hollywood beat us up. And get the one thing Los Angeles is incapable of producing—a decent bagel.

Any emotional hole I had, Ari would try his best to cork and spackle. He was always thoughtful; if I had to travel somewhere, flowers always awaited me. He was protective; once, when the doorbell was stuck and kept ringing and I thought it might be a killer in a hockey mask, he abruptly left work and drove home the wrong way on the 405 freeway to placate me. And if someone was rude to me, he was out for blood. There's nothing more seductive than a man who will duel at dawn for you. Or duel any time of the day, really. Once we were traveling to New York, and the TWA representative informed us our tickets were for a later flight. He said he'd put us on the flight in coach seats. "That's impossible," Ari said, "I paid for first-class tickets." Ari was trying to impress and had spent many miles getting these tickets.

The haughty representative sighed dramatically. "You have coach seats, sir, and even if I had first class, I have a waiting list already filled with devoted platinum TWA flyers. You acquired yours with dividend miles. I'm going to need you to go ahead and step out of the first-class line so I can help people who actually have first-class tickets."

Ari leaned his six-five frame over the ticket podium. "I bought these tickets for this flight! And I'm not leaving until you honor them!"

The TWA representative looked at him with dead eyes. "Could you please leave, and take your white-trash girlfriend with you?"

Wah? Oookkkaayyy, now he'd crossed the line. There was no reason to sling insults, and if so, why smack me? Ari looked right at the guy. "When you were a little boy playing in the sandbox with the other kids, and Timmy wanted to be president and Scooter wanted to be an astronaut, did you actually dream of one day becoming a TWA ticket representative?" He left the man completely deflated. Yes, it was mean. No, I'm not proud of how much I enjoyed it. But never in my life had anyone defended me with such tongue and dagger! And although it was demonstrative and effective, it gradually rendered me unhealthily dependent.

Ari proposed in a castle in Ireland. Yes, a castle, a fortress with stone arches and buttresses that offered weekend tours. He was a man of extremes. We were in Paris
when he shocked me with the news that we were taking a weekend excursion. And with a snap, we were on
Aer Lingus, heading to Dublin. The bastion was down
a long and hilly road dotted with sheep and dandelions.
We had our choice of any of the twenty-four bedrooms,
as he had rented the whole damn thing. We scurried
down one hallway to the next, inspecting the Chinese
bedroom, the red lacquer bedroom, the yellow English
garden bedroom, and so on. We decided on an ivy-
wallpapered room that overlooked a leprechaun green
meadow. In the evening the butler poured us champagne
in front of a roaring fire. Dinner was served at a long oak
banquet table with an ensemble of forks and a festival
of sparkling wineglasses. (Ari had flown in a chef from
Paris. Naturally.) And then, after a sampling of sorbets,
he got down and produced the box. A sparkling emerald
ring was placed on my left hand. It felt heavy, in every
sense of the word. The whole thing was so spectacular, fantastical, and overwhelming. All this for me? Any
girl would feel the luck of the Irish and be Riverdanc-
ing from the dungeon to the tower, but something was
amiss. It was as if I were watching it all on TV and yelling, "You go girl!" to the woman played by me.

When we returned to L.A., we were bombarded
with congratulations and happy wishes. And

as the weeks went on, Ari started to float dates and honeymoon destinations. I wasn't the girl who bought all the *Brides* magazines and tore out photos of bouquets and earmarked pages with colored tabs in Martha Stewart books. I found fault with all possible wedding locations. We couldn't do Martha's Vineyard, my sister had been married there; Manhattan was too busy; Hawaii, too far; London, too cold; Napa, too obvious; Wyoming, too anti-Semitic; and everywhere else was just too . . . wrong. It would be juvenile to chalk this behavior up to being a child of divorce; I didn't have *Kramer vs. Kramer* night terrors and had nothing against the institution of marriage. I just couldn't set a date. Or find a place. Or choose a dress. Like a pacifist in a fighter jet, I couldn't pull the trigger.

I started sleeping fourteen, then sixteen hours a day. I couldn't muster the strength to shower, let alone shave my legs. I stopped returning anyone's calls and ate dry cereal in bed. If someone rang the doorbell, I would scream obscenities out the window like the old lady whose apartment door the police have to finally break down, only to find hundreds of stray dogs eating the remains of Twinkie wrappers.

One Sunday afternoon I finally mustered up my courage. Seated next to Ari on the white linen couch he had presented to me (festooned with a red ribbon) on the day we moved in together, I explained that I had been feeling apathetic and needed to figure out why. Even my rendition of the perfunctory "It's not you, it's me" speech was listless. In fact, I didn't want to be with me; why the hell did he?

I rented a house overlooking the ocean in Santa Monica. The noted documentary filmmaker who owned it was in England interviewing serial killers; with its weather-beaten windowpanes and porches, a mishmash of ceramic pots and plants, and shag rugs doused in coffee and wine stains, it had a timeless appeal. The house begged to blare Joni Mitchell and smelled of huevos rancheros. It gave me the urge to compost.

The only upside to being slightly depressed, for me anyway, is that I lose weight. I don't binge-eat like my friend Polly, who when given any piece of upsetting news will drown herself in a box of White Castle burgers. I just don't eat. That summer I smoked and smoked and smoked, and then, because I turned into an insomniac, I smoked more and at weird hours.

Ari sent me funny news articles or left interior design books and trinkets at my door. I could tell he was anxious for this period of disengagement to be over. And was kind at a time when he should have been asking for back rent, in every sense of the word.

I started blending smoothies (something people who are emotionally constipated do), beach power walking (without the Nike gear), and even had a couple dates. And by dates I mean I went out for a drink with an acquaintance, and if they even tried to hold my hand I would scream rape. I wore bohemian shirts and cropped jeans and bought only organic food. I tried Swedish massage, deep tissue massage, Rolfing and Reiki. Acupuncture, hot stones, Mayan wraps, and algae masks. I drank holistic ointments. I wrote in a leather journal, tried to meditate (which was difficult with *Jerry Springer* on), and read Rilke. Like every white person with dreadlocks and a pierced tongue I saw at the farmer's market, I had become another soul searching for cilantro and myself.

After a month, communication with Ari became sporadic. And when we did speak, he was cryptic about his life or hinted that he couldn't talk because "someone else was there." Suddenly, his detachment from me wasn't sitting well. Yes, I know, I left him, but he was supposed to take to his bed for years until I figured out what I wanted. For me, absence had made the heart grow frantic.

I was picking lint off the sun-faded couch when I decided to check the messages on the answering machine in our New York apartment. Well, realistically, Ari's messages. But I had created the password. And people might be trying to reach me. People who didn't know we'd broken up. There could be messages from doctors with important medical results, or maybe that store had finally received the python cowboy boots I ordered. Or I could have simply been curious for clues about Ari's well-being. Let's face it: women are just better detectives than men. I had a friend who sat on a bench with a thermos of coffee all night watching the entrance of her boyfriend's building because she had a hunch he was cheating on her. She didn't see anything; he hadn't cheated, and she felt imbecilic. But she didn't regret her ludicrous behavior; after all, her mind was eased by the charade. What woman hasn't riffled through her man's e-mails, checked out his ex-girlfriend's Facebook page, or tested him with swabs for STDs while he slept? I called the New York answering machine, punched in the password, and this is what I heard (after a recording about a Filene's basement liquidation sale): "Afternoon sir! This is Veronica from Bahamian Charters! I just wanted to confirm your private charter this weekend for you and your wife!"

I felt like a Chihuahua after the neighborhood bully lit the firecracker in its ass. I started hyperventilating. For a second I thought I was going to black out, and smash through the coffee table like Sean Young in *No Way Out*. But then I realized that I couldn't die because I had just been served too much drama to sort out. What the hell was he doing in the Bahamas? It seemed like such a non sequitur. He had no connection to that island—or any other island, for that matter; he freckled and burned! And a private charter? What was a private charter? Was it a plane or a boat or a school? Was he continuing his education in a nonsectarian community-based public school? If it was a plane, why was it private? It sounded so sneaky and immoral. And who the fuck was this wife? I was the wife! The would-have-been wife! The could-have-been wife! No way could he be serious about anyone so soon! It had only been six weeks! . . . I racked my brain. Was it the writer's assistant who dressed like a prostitute? The platinum blond dog walker who always loitered to talk to him in the driveway? My mind was a Jackson Pollock of minuscule women's faces. I started to cry, which quickly escalated into screaming and wailing. I was unraveling at high speed. Like the evil Nazi in *Raiders of the Lost Ark* whose face melts off after he witnesses the opening of the ark. It felt just like that.

I grabbed the phone, concentrated long enough to stop my fingers from shaking, and dialed my mother. I needed to hear the voice I had been connected with since I was prenatal. A voice that was stronger and more resilient than my own. My mother, Muffie.

When she answered, I couldn't speak; I just gave out a primal, guttural howl.

"What's going on?" Her voice was calm, but I noted concern in her inflection. I tried to muster the lucidity to explain. I screamed about the Bahamas and the voice mail, the other woman, the deceit, my mistake, my regret, my fear, then more about the mystery girl and how I had destroyed my life. I shuddered and shook and nearly suffocated on my inhales, like a toddler whose lollipop has been snatched from its mouth. My cheeks were soaked in tears and snot and saliva.

After an eternity of emotional unwinding, I decided to let my mother speak. She had always been the voice of reason, the fixer, the cleaner, the person who knew how to take hold of the reins and drive the carriage home.

She sighed. "Sweetheart," she began in her smooth, assuring voice, and then she took a long pause. "Nobody goes to the Bahamas in July!"

———— ✧ ————

Yes, my mother's name is Muffie, but don't let the name fool you. She doesn't wear headbands and Belgian loafers; she doesn't winter in Palm Beach or summer in Vineyard Haven. She doesn't have any needlepoint pillows with inane sayings like, "Dogs are just children in fur coats," and she doesn't collect porcelain figurines. The name Muffie itself conjures up a plethora of stereotypes that I can eradicate with two simple statements: one, she doesn't drink; and two, there is no more money. Sure, years ago great-great-grandparents invested well in Ford Motor Company and Standard Oil and relatives were able to live in style and skate through an economic downturn, but those days are gone. The money has since been invested badly, embezzled by greedy spouses, or drunk away. The only visible trace of any WASP heritage is the name. And the lineage. And the ethics, theology, and ideology. And the fact that she was raised in Boston, went to boarding school and Smith, and twice married men from Harvard. Plus, she's never peed in the shower.

This Muffie, my mother, is strong and determined. "Balls!" said the Queen. "If I had them I'd be King!" She has worked her whole life and during any down time wrote a book, started a company, or curated an exhibit about the women who formed this country. And in her spare time cleaned out a garage or had a yard sale on the hottest day in Maine or drove ten hours to Cape Cod with four screaming kids. If anyone were to write the "I know how to have it all, find balance, live a fulfilling life, lose weight, aha moment chicken soup, live your best life on ten dollars a day" book, it's Muffie.

Everybody knows my mother. Even if they've never met my mother, they know my mother. I could be at the American embassy in Moscow doing shots of vodka with an antipropaganda documentarian from Siberia or scraping barnacles off the bottom of a Spinola Bay boat with a toothless lobsterman, and I will undoubtedly hear, "Please give your mother my love." The maid who cleans the First Lady's toilet knows my mom; the illegal Peruvian plumber knows my mom; the man who produced *Charlie's Angels* knew my mom. She is beloved by all gay men, who in my opinion constitute the world's most discerning judges of character. She is democratic and liberal, marched down Main Street for her beliefs, fought for civil rights, campaigned for all the Kennedy brothers, and managed to maintain democratic status in the Reagan White House. She has helped alcoholic friends get sober by walking them up and down the beaches of Cape Cod and played Monopoly on the carpet with financial tycoons. And won. She never wears makeup, but always has impeccably manicured toes. We have the exact same singular chin hair. She could invade Poland on a snorting white horse, but breaks into tears over a splinter. Her favorite lunch is sliced tomatoes on bread, deviled eggs, and iced tea. You can bribe her into anything if you can produce a hot fudge sundae. The only things my mother can cook are English muffins and crème caramel. She will choose a bath over a shower, a play over a movie, and the ocean over a pool. She has saved herself from intense pain in her life with strong, pulled-up bootstraps and terrifying organizational skills. She has the legs for tennis, the grace for skiing, and such high-arched eyebrows they could bring the Supreme Court to their knees.

My mother has Givenchy gowns she bought at a Saks sale (or for all I know, were created for her by Givenchy himself) in the closet next to frayed evening jackets she excitedly scored at Goodwill. She doesn't believe in hedonism, loathes ostentation, and will buy boxed wine from Costco over Châteaux Margaux if it means more money for the Boston Museum. She didn't grow up in the age of private planes, Pilates instructors, and hiring Ke$ha to play at birthday parties. She finds the new world self-serving and indulgent. She constantly screams "Hello?" at her iPhone before hitting the answer button.

I have spent half my life rebelling against my upbringing, as most people do. If my mother had been a hooker, I'd be a Rhodes Scholar today. If my mother had been a Rhodes Scholar, I'd be a hooker. I was once asked by *Playboy* to show skin in an issue they were doing on funny women. The exciting thing for me was not that they thought it was even feasible to feature me naked in their august publication, but the exhilaration I would get from telling my mother. "*Playboy* is offering me one hundred thousand dollars to pose naked," I announced gleefully. (It was actually more like ten thousand, but the money was irrelevant.)

There was one of her famous long pauses. "Well, I will pay you a hundred and ONE thousand dollars not to pose naked."

Of course, I never intended to even consider the offer, more for aesthetic reasons than out of any moral qualms: I knew what I looked like naked, and it wasn't going to sell many magazines. In any case, Phyllis Diller took my page.

CHAPTER TWO

mama, can you hear me?

When I was four years old, we moved from a modest family home into an immodest four-story brick house situated on a dead-end street. There were thick woods to the right, and the driveway to the British embassy to the left. To an adult it was quiet, exclusive, and swank, but to a child it was eerie and lonely, the woods riddled with ghosts, goblins, and faceless zombie children on a quest to eat my soul through decapitation (was this just my fear?). It was a lonely existence on Whitehaven Street; the whole concept of *Sesame Street* and the always upbeat people in the neighborhood was lost on me. I never got to experience hanging on the stoop with multiracial kids, kicking the can with the neighborhood gang, or frolicking in the fire hydrant sprinklers. I could walk the length of our street (about a quarter mile) without ever seeing a single person. Much less a freakishly tall yellow bird.

The house was in a section of Washington called Embassy Row, where every country in the world has a residence and representation in the nation's capital. It's like frat houses, with the cool ones (Italy and France), who threw parties like recruitment week at William and Mary, and the lame ones (Zimbabwe and Sri Lanka), who'd maybe get a few interns from the UN who had to BYOB their own Red Bulls. When I was a teenager, during the Iran hostage crisis, there were so many protests right outside our door, we could have been living in Tehran. It has never been proven, but I know I saw a Khomeini supporter in our kitchen stealing cheese.

At that time in my life, I abhorred sleepovers. Why would I want another kid breaking off my Barbie legs and forcing me to stay up until midnight discussing which acne-faced and annoying boy I would kiss if there was a gun to my head? I never got past why someone who had a gun would choose to use it to unearth my hidden third-grade desires. At nine years old, you were supposed to beg for sleepovers, so I did, the same way in college you were supposed to have a tattoo, so I did (but with a Sharpie). I dreaded packing my sleeping bag, toothbrush, and clean underwear. As a child of divorce, I saw it as just one more dysfunctional family I had to stay with.

I had a best friend in second through fourth grade named Constance. We wore identical outfits, wrote secret notes without words, and conducted endless phone conversations without talking. It seemed natural that my first sleepover would be with her. You know the movie *Carrie*? It paled in comparison to a night at Constance's house. The problem being, her mother was nuts: she was erratic, had hallucinations, and spoke in tongues. The woman should have been a leader at a witches' coven, not the PTA. One night Constance and I were getting ready for our first girl/ boy party. We had spent all day pairing the correct bell-bottom corduroy with the appropriate Danskin turtleneck, Hush Puppies with the matching headband, and earrings that didn't accentuate braces. We started blow-drying our hair at two o'clock in the afternoon and applying lip gloss at four. It was a big night, a preteen's prom, just when the hormones were starting to kick in, here was a platform upon which to exercise them, in the concrete form of Spin the Bottle and Five Minutes in the Closet, bathroom, freezer, heaven, wherever.

Constance's mother drove us the twenty minutes to the party, which was being hosted by Stewart, a pipsqueak in a rugby shirt and penny loafers, eager for his first kiss (Stewart is now a U.S. senator). As we reached the ranch-style house, Constance's mother pulled the car to an abrupt halt. She whipped her head around and, with eyes beaming red, screamed, "I know what you're going to do in there! You think I don't know? You are little whores!!!" With that, she stepped on the gas and we were speeding back to

Constance's house, where we were berated and sent to bed.

Fearing I would be forced to pray to Jesus Christ in a candlelit basement the next time, I decided I would no longer sleep over at Constance's house. In fact, I decided I would no longer even drive by Constance's house. If we were going to make Jiffy Pop popcorn and color in our fashion books, it would be in the safety of my own home. With chaperones who didn't say things like, "Pimples are the Lord's way of chastising you."

I decided to give the sleepover frenzy one more chance. Constance's mother finally acquiesced, and Constance came over for my first hosted sleepover at our house at the end of our creepy street. We had our favorite meal, spaghetti and meatballs, vanilla ice cream, and Welch's grape juice blended with ice. And we were allowed to eat it in pajamas. Everyone in the house was far more excited about this playdate than I was; they acted like I was experiencing a major rite of passage. "What a big night! A SLLLEEEEEEPPPPPP-OOOOVVEERRRRRR!!!!" my older sister kept saying. My mother was in a sparkling Armani gown, my stepfather in a tuxedo, as they watched us slurp up the last noodles. They were off to a dinner, but before they left they wanted to fan the sleepover excitement.

"Look at you guys having spaghetti on your sleepover!" Really, it became a bigger event than my wedding night.

Finally, by eight o'clock, my parents were out, my older siblings were out, and Constance and I were alone in the house. Well, except for our babysitter Elizabeth, but she was in the basement with a cigar watching *Barney Miller* on top volume, so we were essentially alone.

My mother's room was always the center of our universe. If we were sick, we would sweat and vomit in her bed; if we were sad, we would cry and bury ourselves under her pillows. Any important news was headlined from her bed—things like "Your father is having an affair" and "Your brother's been arrested climbing the outside of the Washington Cathedral." I have carried on the tradition by designating my bed a free-floating lift raft for both my daughters. In fact, we would all get by perfectly well with just a king mattress and a hot plate.

So Constance and I curled up on my mom's bed with a stack of comic books and a box of Ding Dongs. I yearned to be in my lower bunk in matching night-gowns with my miniature dachshund, Max, but instead powered through the dreaded sleepover ritual.

The phone rang. Constance darted toward it and, even though I reminded her that I never answered the phone because I never got calls, Constance picked up. "Hello?" She stared at me in silence and then slammed the receiver down.

"What?" Constance dug herself under the down comforter. "Who was it?" She ignored me. I ate another Ding Dong.

The phone rang again. Constance picked it up before the second ring. "Hello?" There was a long pause, and she hung up. She screamed loudly and insanely. "Some man was on the phone! He said he is going to kill us tonight!"

My heart was beating so hard it almost leaped out of my ballerina nightgown, taking my inner child with it. "What do you mean? What did he say?"

Constance pulled the sheets over her head, and from under the covers I heard a muffled, "I don't know who it is! He just said he was going to kill us!"

I had never seen a slasher film in its entirety or read the *New York Post*, so I wasn't savvy about the real-world horrors lurking outside, but I did have an active and vibrant imagination. My brain could host its own Wes Craven scare fest unprompted. I visualized a beady-eyed man wearing a black leather jacket (like all bad guys) with a large chain saw in his hand hacking up Constance's body. (I never thought of it as my body because it's always scarier to witness the crime than to be the victim.)

I climbed over the mound of Constance and grabbed the phone. I dialed 411. "British Embassy. Yes, residence."

Within minutes, the police sirens and floodlights had transformed our dead end street into an Aerosmith concert. There was pounding on the front door, and when I opened it, the British ambassador stood anxiously in his navy striped pajamas and Burberry raincoat. The embassy guards and D.C. cops started searching the house, along with two rabidly sniffing German shepherds. I cowered on the front steps with the ambassador and a female police officer with zero maternal instincts. Constance stayed in the lump until a cop escorted her out to the front yard with the rest of us. You would have thought it was a bomb scare at the UN or the Barneys Warehouse sale.

My parents pulled up in time to witness all the commotion. I remember my mother running up the driveway, her dress billowing behind her. There was a reaction of relief—nothing was stolen, and I was still breathing—and embarrassment—the ambassador was standing in our front lawn at midnight in his PJs. Elizabeth the babysitter had fallen asleep during *The Rockford Files* and had snored through the whole show.

I still couldn't shake the fact that there was a man somewhere out there, hiding in an embassy Dumpster, plotting my demise. I slept next to my mother that night in a position that ensured I maintained contact with 90 percent of her body mass at all times. Constance slept upstairs in my room on the upper bunk. My stepfather couldn't handle two kicking and thrashing nine-year-olds in his bed. Plus, they had never been fans of Constance's; he felt it was enough he didn't charge her for meals.

I could hear my stepfather's teeth grinding and felt my mother's last muscular twitch before she fell into a deep slumber. I had almost nodded off when Constance cracked open the door, blinding me with the hall light, and slipped into the room. She came close to my face and whispered, "It was a wrong number."

I rubbed my eyes. "What?"

She whispered again, "I made it up. It was a wrong number." She smiled like she had informed me I was soaking in Palmolive and crept out. My first and last sleepover until my college years, and even those I would tiptoe out of before dawn.

CHAPTER THREE

just a spoon full of something

My mother can juggle more plates in the air than the androgynous clown in Cirque du Soleil. When I was between the ages of five and twelve, she was particularly industrious. Her second husband, whom she married four years after she and my father divorced, was a British foreign correspondent who was so steeped in the Washington scene there was no getting him out, like blood on silk. He was covering the JFK, LBJ, and Nixon administrations, so access to the inner sanctum was crucial. Consequently, our home became soiree central.

I recall clutching the back of Henry Kissinger's neck as he hauled me around the deep end of the pool. Only in Washington could a man paddle around like a tortoise in a heated swimming pool with a giggling five-year-old while he was simultaneously bombing Cambodia. But what did I know, he had a wide back.

———— ⌒⌒ ————

There were grandiose cocktail parties where my little sister and I, adorned in matching nightgowns, would pass peanuts that our sticky fingers had played with in the kitchen. There were always the same hors d'oeuvres, which I still crave from time to time— a round piece of white toast with a pastry squirt of baked mayonnaise and Parmesan cheese. A fistful of those, and we'd call it dinner. There's a fine line between WASP victuals and white-trash cuisine.

When a government official was a guest, he would be accompanied by a band of humorless Secret Service agents in dark suits. When I was eight, I had a miniature dachshund named Max who was my soul mate, my guru, my captain, and my priest. My political prejudice toward the Nixon administration was not brought about by Watergate, illegal wiretaps, or the Vietnam War—no, it was their conduct toward my dog. (And by the way, this is by and large how I still judge people today.) One night when the Secretary of State was over for a leg of lamb and heated discussion about the Soviet Union and North Korea, he had the audacity to have Max locked in a cage. I fumed: He was one of the leaders of the free world, surrounded by enemies and potential assassins, and he chose to imprison a puppy the size of an evening clutch and as cunning as a melon ball? And if that wasn't appalling enough, a Secret Service man was posted outside my bedroom door. I can understand securing the exits and blocking basement doors, but an eight-year-old girl's room with matching blush pink tulip wallpaper and curtains? What was I going to do? Leap out of bed in my nightgown and stab the Secretary of State with my Snoopy toothbrush?

My stepfather's sixtieth birthday party was an extravaganza, complete with diaphanous white tent and multitudinous candles. Max was in a cage, per usual, and I had spent most of the afternoon with Betsy, a zaftig cook hired for special occasions, who was making individual apricot soufflés. I loved Betsy not just because she was a comforting butterball of a woman, but because she had no filter; she would just say what she thought at the exact moment she thought it. If my mother ran by in curlers, fretting about the seating, Betsy would mumble, "She's running around so much like a crazy, I should have her whip these egg whites instead of this beater." Betsy would sit on a stool all night, sticking her fingers in every bowl, plate, and platter. And she was always disgusted with everything and everyone. "Who are all those people out there with too much perfume?" She would pick up a chop. "This ain't cooked! This poor animal's going to get up and walk off the table."

I had rehearsed my endearing rendition of "Animal Crackers" to perform that evening. I assumed if Shirley Temple could steal people's hearts by singing and tap-dancing, then I could seduce my stepfather into accepting me as his own flesh and blood even without the curls. Or the talent. The tables were one big blur of glowing lights, and I couldn't make out any faces, with one exception. Henry Kissinger watched me chasse, grand jeté, and pas de bourrée my needy little butt off without even the hint of a smile. He stared me down with an expression borrowed from the evil child catcher in *Chitty Chitty Bang Bang*. I ended with a ta-da pose: arms in the air, back arched, an all-teeth smile. There was enthusiastic applause from the crowd and erratic clapping from Kissinger (it looked more like he was trying to kill a mosquito). I moved in for an encore, but was led back into the kitchen with Betsy. She mumbled something about me making an ass out of myself as she ran her finger around the icing of the gargantuan white chocolate cake.

If there wasn't a fete at our house, there was definitely a fete somewhere else. My mother and stepfather were elegantly coiffed and bejeweled most nights of the week. They also traveled a fair amount. As a result of their rigorous social schedule, we were awarded a live-in babysitter. We started with Jessica, a Brandeis student with a pixie haircut and enormous breasts, so enormous she told me she could never find a bathing suit that fit, which became very clear during my sailing lessons. Jessica stayed with us the summer I was seven at our house in Plymouth, Massachusetts, while my mother and stepfather were in China for a few months. I spent my time hitting a tennis ball against a cracked backboard and anticipating the chimes of the ice cream truck. It was a blissful summer, but for two things: I missed my mom, and there was an overpopulation of sand flies. In the fall Jessica had to return to college, but not without an irreplaceable going-away gift. My older brother confessed to us, years later, that one sultry summer night Jessica crawled into bed with him, pulled off his race car pajamas, and stole his virginity. He was fourteen, and the size of one of her boobs. In retrospect it made sense; Jessica and my brother spent hours behind locked doors while she "tutored him" in algebra. He should have been Bill Gates today, given all the hours they logged studying algorithms and polynomials. He still failed algebra twice.

When Fiona was born, my mother chose an authentic British nanny named Julia from an agency in London that still serviced in uniforms and little crisp hats. I was always amused because as my sister learned to talk, she did so with a strong British accent: water was "wattah" and Mommy was "Mummy." Julia was the kind of disciplinarian who believed in a tight schedule, clean clothes, and brisk walks no matter what the temperature. Fiona was indoctrinated into an important work ethic during the potty-training years, which is why she went on to Brown University and I to Bard College. Julia was our Mary Poppins, until one day she turned in her resignation. She was marrying a successful financial adviser, not the chimney sweep. And she was off to have babies she wouldn't be paid to love.

Greta was German. Never hire a German woman to care for your kids. You wouldn't want an Italian working on your car or an Irish lass cooking your meal. I've never admired the German language, least of all when it's screamed at me from a foot away. When she ordered us to do our homework, it felt like we were going to invade Latvia. Greta was eventually fired for her undemonstrative outlook and tyrannical views toward punishment (to her, *Triumph of the Will* was a Disney movie), but the real reason she was discharged had to do with a Thanksgiving incident in which she tore a leg off the turkey before it was set on the table, and continued eating it as, like an SS captain, she yelled at us to wash our hands. It wasn't so much that she had destroyed the symbol of the holiday by ripping off its limb as it was a chilling metaphor for what she was capable of when it came to child care.

My stepfather was a notorious bachelor before he married my mother in his early fifties. He'd had his share of the ladies; on the wall of his study he hung a photo of Marilyn Monroe in a leotard eyeing him lasciviously as if he were a six-carat diamond or a bottle of pills. During his bachelorhood, he was looked after by Elizabeth Morrison, who cleaned for him, collected mail for him, and gave disapproving looks to women searching for their heels in the dawn light. Elizabeth was a hefty African American woman who wore a white nurse's uniform. In her younger days she had been a nurse, and she found it easier to simply stick with the same outfit week in, week out than go through the imbecilic routine of trying to decide what to wear every day. Even in the summer when she would take us to the beach, she wore the nurse uniform, black support hose, and white shoes. She hated the beach and used to mutter, "Look at everybody just sitting in the sun. Black people want to be white, white people want to be black." I loved her gravelly voice, the result of fifty years of bourbon and cigarettes. And Elizabeth loved poker. She refused to get down on the carpet with a box of Barbies or create collages with rubber stamps; in fact, she didn't like to do much, least of all crafts, but if you flashed a deck of cards, within seconds you'd be at the kitchen table with a bowl of Chex mix, watching her inhale Pall Malls like a desperado for hours on end.

Elizabeth gave off an aura of fortitude, perhaps the byproduct of a tough childhood or some hard knocks along the way. One afternoon when I came home from school, expecting the usual tongue bath from my beloved Max, I was instead greeted by a deathly quiet house and Elizabeth solemnly standing in the doorway. She fixed me with a stern look. "Max is dead. It doesn't matter how [he'd been hit by a car], he dead. You can cry and cry, which ain't going to bring him back, or just move on now." I spent the afternoon playing seven-card stud and biting my lower lip. If I missed my mom, Elizabeth would say, "She's coming back! But if you keep moping around like that, why would she want to?" And when she tucked me into bed, she would turn out the light with a simple, "All right. Good night." When my brother was giving her lip, she would twist a wet towel and try to thwack his thighs; she wouldn't take shit from anybody, especially not an awkwardly tall, long-haired teenage boy with acne and doped-up eyes. I loved Elizabeth. She lived with our family on and off until I was ten and then went off to live with a relative; she had gotten too old for the antics of a family of obstreperous kids, incontinent dogs, and itinerant parents. I hope for her sake that relative resided in Vegas.

I think my mother hired each babysitter as a reaction to the predecessor. If one was too loose, the next one was too strict, and so on. One of the most baffling decisions my mother ever made (besides working in a Republican White House) was hiring Brandelyn, a three-hundred-pound Mormon from Utah. My mother must have found her in the Church of Jesus Christ of the Latter-Day Saints Craigslist. I'm not a fatist, but somebody who is caring for young children should be able to at least walk. And not wear powder blue polyester pantsuits while battling a body odor problem. Brandelyn would bathe my little sister and me every night, scrubbing our bodies with loofahs. "You have to get the dirt out of your bodies and your minds," she would say as she scoured our necks raw. And there was never enough talk about the Lord. "The Lord wouldn't like it if you ate that cookie before dinner, the Lord doesn't like children that scream, the Lord damns people to hell if they don't floss. . . ." She did a horrific job of selling us on Jesus; he was more didactic and ominous than any parent I knew, including Mrs. Williams, the Chinese mother who hit my classmate Adele with a stick while she practiced violin. Brandelyn's fate was sealed when she flushed my gerbil, Bubbles, down the toilet because she decided it was rabid. Bubbles was from a reputable pet store, but apparently the Lord deemed it so. We draw the line when you start killing family.

And then there was Summer. She looked like the Joan Armatrading album cover she was always playing. She was skinny, had a huge Afro, and wore bell-bottom jeans and crocheted sweaters. And she was beyond cool. There was no bedtime, dinner was craving-based, and undergarments were strictly optional. Summer was popular and beloved; the doorbell rang at all hours of the day and night. I thought we had finally found a staple in our life, a surrogate mom, friend, and confidant, all embodied in a woman who looked like she jumped off a *Mod Squad* lunch box. But six months into the job, Summer was abruptly fired; she had been (allegedly) dealing heroin out of the house. Yup, just another nanny hustling junk, selling pie, flipp'n sack from behind an Easy-Bake Oven.

And then there were none. I think my mother decided, before our home became a crack den, that we would no longer have babysitters live in. She threw in the towel and decided to just raise us herself.

I had my eldest daughter in a heat wave in Washington, D.C., the summer of 2002. She was a few weeks old when I started the search for the babysitter. I tried word of mouth, referrals, and the local paper. I decided to cover all my bases and pulled a phone number tab off a self-made nanny advertisement at the corner pharmacy. I hired Lala the day I called, mostly because I felt like a hen flapping around in the "I don't know how to do this" motherhood pen. She was from the Philippines, legal, and had raised six children herself; I thought I had struck goo-goo-ga-ga gold.

That afternoon Lala pulled the baby off my nipple and said, "Oh Mommmmyyyyy . . . I take baby to the park."

Naturally, I thought she knew much more than

me when it came to child rearing, the Pacific ring of fire, and how to cook milkfish. "Um, okay," I timidly answered, buttoning my blouse, "but be back in thirty minutes, because I think she's still hungry and it's ninety degrees out." She nodded and laughed, exposing a mouth full of dental mishaps. The amazing thing about women from the Philippines is they're ageless. Lala could have been eighteen or eighty, there was no way of telling: their skin stays the same, their silky hair—the only clue is the teeth. When a Filipino woman takes her teeth out and puts them in a cup of water, she's over forty.

An hour went by . . . then two . . . then three. I called my husband in a panic. "She's been kidnapped!" I ran sweating up and down the stairs, balancing a breast pump and the phone. Like a Vietnam vet who hears a car backfire, I flashed back to the many babysitters from my youth and feared I was starting my own line of adventures in babysitting hell.

Three and a half hours later, Lala came home with the sweaty and parched baby. Needless to say, she was fired immediately; a neighbor later told me they had seen her at the park canoodling with a man while the stroller sat there under a tree. SHE LEFT MY STARVING BABY FOR THREE HOURS DURING A HEAT WAVE! I spit on her name.

After Lala's one day of employment, we hired a baby nurse named Juju. My eldest is almost nine years old, and Juju still lives with us. I have no idea of her age, but she's never abandoned my children out in a heatwave and she loves crabbing with raw chicken necks as much as me. As General Electric would say, "She brings good things to life."

And Juju will live with us forever—even if she sells dope out of the house!

CHAPTER FOUR

don't look back

When my older sister was seventeen, she underwent spinal fusion surgery. She had scoliosis from birth, and my parents had hoped a back brace would mend it. But she never wore her back brace. She would leave for school, sneak around the back of the house, stash the brace in the garage, and race onto the school bus. The surgical procedure fused her vertebrae together so her spine would be straight, and the brace could permanently live behind the pile of firewood and mice droppings.

I was twelve years old the summer Sissy had surgery at Mass. General Hospital. It was a sweltering and sticky July in Boston, and I remember living on chips from a vending machine and lying on the plastic-tiled hospital floor talking to my sister while she was suspended upside down in a medieval bed contraption. At the time I didn't realize the extent of such major surgery. (The only other time I had been in a hospital was when I was born, on a gurney in the hallway during a blizzard, so my initial reaction to being there was to feel cold and lonely.) Both my divorced parents were there, trading seats, conferring with doctors, and fetching coffee. Sometimes my sister would scream so loudly I could hear it down the hallway in the waiting room, where I'd be working on my Mad Libs. It was usually a sign the morphine drip had run dry.

The hospital had a distinct smell, a combination of pudding, Lysol, and piss. (Do hospitals have a rule against potpourri?) My sister couldn't move for weeks and had to poop in a bag, which was both fascinating and repulsive to me. For that reason alone I never wanted to have surgery. Although as a middle-aged woman, I might put up with pooping in a bag for a good face lift.

When I wasn't trying to amuse myself with popping rubber gloves and stacking pill cups at the nurses' station, Fiona and I stayed in our house in Plymouth. The modest house, with a stunning view of the public beach, was just over an hour's car ride from the hospital. Back then, Plymouth was a tiny village that survived off saltwater taffy sales and tours run by adults dressed up as pilgrims and Indians, who crushed corn and sharpened arrows with rocks. They weren't allowed to break character, so if you asked a pilgrim where the gift shop was, she would answer, "Thou dost not know from what thou speakest." ("Yes, but doesn't thee drive a Pinto and babysitteth us sometimes?") I still remember seeing an Indian

Squanto complete with loincloth sharing a cigarette and Dunkin' Donuts coffee with Captain John Smith behind the Wampanoag barn.

Fiona and I would spend the days in Plymouth with a mélange of long-haired, long-legged teenage babysitters in bikinis and straw hats named Jody, Darcy, and Liz. Down the hill from our house was the Eel River Beach Club. It was named for the begrimed canal of backwash between the club and the ocean, which housed slimy eels that boys threw rocks at or tried to catch in the janitor's bucket. The only prerequisite for being a member of the club was you had to live in the town. If you lived kinda near, that was okay too. The club consisted of a cracked saltwater pool, one tennis court with grass growing through the tar, and a snack shack with a cook who was always out of supplies. We would spend the whole day there, dozing on our Marimekko beach towels on the hot cement, perfecting our knee flips in the saltwater pool, and slurping melting Creamsicles. The highlight, when it was really hot, was when we would pop tar bubbles on the paved parking lot.

The nights were peaceful; with the window open you could hear the crashing of the ocean waves, which lulled me to sleep—until that summer when the movie *Jaws* came out. After that, my windows were permanently sealed shut; I was too young, and the film traumatized me for life. My brother and his long-haired stoner friends took me opening night. These are the sorts of mishaps that occur when your mother is away changing bedpans. After the movie we all went to the beach, where I was catatonic, held hostage to their fake shark attacks in the moonlit ocean. I didn't take a bath for two years and still won't swim in water above the waist, and that includes swimming pools and koi ponds. Sissy missed the *Jaws* phenomenon that summer, but considering she was ripped apart by the teeth of great white surgical instruments, it was a blessing.

I used to lie on my single bed during those summer days for hours. When you're young, your mind isn't bogged down by questions about discovering your true self, preventing cancer, and liquidating assets; you can obsess about when you'll sprout breasts for weeks on end. My only fleeting concerns (aside from my sharkophobia) were for Sissy and for my mother, who slept in a hospital chair for weeks. There's a scene in the movie *Terms of Endearment* that was pulled from that summer. In the scene Debra Winger is dying and in great pain, and her mother, played by Shirley Mac-Laine, runs to the nurses' station, screaming, "Give my daughter the shot!" For me it's like watching a home movie.

———— ⌁ ————

My mother decided that when my sister was released from the hospital, we would all stay in a rented house up in Marion, near Buzzard's Bay. Sissy was going to be encased in a full body cast for six months, and Marion was breezy and temperate. My mother rented an ambulance to transport Sissy up there. At the time I assumed this was so that in the event of a postsurgical complication, the medical technician would be on hand. But in hindsight, I think my mother just didn't want to have to stop at red lights.

The Marion rental was a small white clapboard house with windowpanes of original glass that distorted the landscape and faces that passed by. Sissy spent most of the day horizontal. The body cast extended from her chin to below her pelvis. Fiona and I would break up the monotony of her day by taking extra-long Q-tips, dipping them in rubbing alcohol, and digging under the plaster to relieve itches. Fiona was young enough that a piece of string could occupy her for hours. Sissy was despondent with boredom.

One afternoon Sissy was particularly agitated. She was crying and banging her cast against the wall molding and narrow doorways, much like a toddler trying to walk with a bucket on his head. Fiona was busy still playing with string, and I was on my twenty-sixth pastel drawing of a clamshell. Sissy stomped into the kitchen. "I can't live like this anymore! I'm running away!"

My mother stopped snapping peas. "Okay, okay, simmer down . . . you want some ginger ale?" The comfort elixir in our house.

Sissy's fist hit the side of the refrigerator. "NO! I'm leaving! I'm running away!" And like that, she threw open the screen door and started waddling down the front path. My mother walked into the living room, where I was spread out on the floor surrounded by paper, pastels, paint, and a bunch of clamshells. "Go with your sister."

I looked up at her. "I don't want to run away!"

My mother tapped her foot on the knotty pine floor. "Please run away with your sister! I don't want her out there alone!"

"But I don't want to run away!"

"I'm asking you nicely, now go!"

I was getting irritated. "I don't want to run away, Mom! I want to stay home! I'm happy!"

At this point she snapped, "GET OUT!"

I stood up in a huff, grabbed a Channel Thirteen tote bag, and filled it with a can of tuna, a bottle of juice, two apricot fruit rolls, and a spoon. I slammed the screen door as I ventured out to find my sister lurching like Frankenstein through a cluster of pine trees. It's hard enough to swallow your mother forcing you to run away, but when I finally caught up with Sissy, she screamed at me to go home. I considered running away on my own at this point, but knew my mother would invest all her efforts in finding Sissy first, and I'd be in Tijuana doing tricks with a donkey before anyone realized I wasn't at breakfast. So I followed Sissy from twenty feet away like some nymph stalker. We were in a part of Massachusetts that was foreign to us, so I just followed her path and prayed it would lead to a Howard Johnson. Finally, as dusk began to fall, we collided with an actual paved road, an occasional car whizzing by. Sissy stormed along the side of the road and I scampered behind, giving passing cars the "don't ask" look. I was seething. We were in danger of missing *The Partridge Family*, and I had forgotten a can opener for the tuna.

We walked for yards. Sissy finally stopped and rested her cast against a stone wall surrounding a cemetery. A small cemetery, probably one family's worth of deceased. I was starving and ready to face the consequences of going home for food and shelter. "I'm never going home," Sissy huffed, trying to catch her breath.

"You know it's Friday night! We're going to miss *The Brady Bunch*, *Partridge Family*, and *Love, American Style!*" I was on the verge of bursting into tears. I felt guilty; here was my sister, who had just had her back split open like a chicken breast, with a metal rod skewering her like a shish kebab, and my shallow universe was shattered by the idea of not hearing a family of bad shag haircuts belt out, "I think I love you." Even though Sissy was tall, blond, and very beautiful, she didn't deserve that horrific operation. Well, maybe her svelte legs merited a root canal, but not this.

"What do I have to do for us to go home?" I asked as Sissy looked away. Silence. And then: "If you can make me laugh, I'll go home."

I repeated the terms, so we were crystal clear: "If I make you laugh, you will go home?"

"Yes," she snorted. For the record, Sissy hadn't cracked a smile in eight months.

It's difficult to be funny on demand. In the woods. Without pay. I'm sure if Richard Pryor had been in my position, he wouldn't have jumped up on a mound of dirt and delivered a thirty-minute set, in Massachusetts, with no crack.

I zipped across the road to the cemetery, because where better to find yucks than a plot of dead people? I looked around for props and anything that would trigger some creative initiative. Sissy stared at me like she was watching the Nuremberg trials. I found an unused black garbage bag caught in a branch. I hid behind the largest tombstone (clearly the money-maker of the family), out of view from Sissy and the road. I stripped down to my white undies with pink faded bows. I used my teeth to make holes in the top and sides of the bag and pulled it over my head. I gathered a bunch of twigs and meticulously wrapped them around small bunches of hair—instant forest hot rollers. The ground was moist enough to mix a muddy concoction, and I rubbed it on my face like Trish McEvoy cover-up. I put leaves between my toes, weeds around my neck, and a dandelion behind one ear. I was Bigfoot and Nell's child.

I popped up from the grave like a stripper from a cake. At that precise moment two cars were driving by. The Volvo screeched to a halt, causing the VW bug to brake abruptly and careen to the side. Suddenly windows were down, and even a golden retriever was gawking. It was show time. I pranced around like a member of some esoteric Martha Graham dance troupe, occasionally berating a squirrel or pretending to seduce a birch tree. I was so committed to the role that I didn't realize there was a traffic jam piling up on the road. As I broke character and absorbed the absurdity of my surroundings and the borderline psychotic lack of inhibition, I caught Sissy in my peripheral vision—she had fallen over. Laughing. I'd like to think it was my performance, which will never be seen by the Academy, but for her it was my complete abandonment of self respect. The fact that I would sacrifice all dignity just to get home to the Friday TV lineup was unfathomable to her. Sissy laughed so hard she peed in her voluminous linen pants, which provided us with an even more compelling reason to go home.

When we finally hobbled through the door, my mother and Fiona were eating scrambled eggs. My mother took Sissy to her room and changed and comforted her. Afterward, we all convened in the living room just in time to catch Marcia Brady receiving her corsage. Fiona was tying string around her legless doll, my mother brushed Sissy's flaxen hair, and I sat mesmerized by a TV family of six children who lived a perfect suburban life, complete with a well-groomed dog and a wisecracking housekeeper who probably worked for free (just being part of the bunch was enough). They lived an ideal childhood with inconsequential hardships that were without fail resolved in twenty-two minutes. They didn't have divorce or episodes of madness in a cemetery, and unless I missed that episode, none of those kids ever spent time on a morphine drip.

CHAPTER FIVE

girls, interrupted

For generations in my family, when a child turned thirteen he or she was shipped off to boarding school. It wasn't questioned, it wasn't a choice, you just went. My parents went to boarding school, as did their parents and their parents' parents—all the way back to the Pilgrims. The Pilgrims prepped by debating the Bible, freezing root vegetables, and bullying Indians.

My older brother and sister were dispatched before me, and it seemed innocuous enough. As they weren't around during their teenage years, there were no rooms that smelled like pot (except for school breaks), band practice in the garage, or make-out parties in the basement to corrupt me. However, my sister did get suspended from school for having beer in her room. She was sentenced to a week back home. I remember it being a crisis on par with Watergate, which we had just lived through. There were endless hushed discussions: "What should we do?" "Oh, God! How could this have happened"? I mean, it was an Amstel Light, not a human skull. But it did make prep school seem devious and exciting. So, naturally, I wanted in.

I picked an all-girls school. First big mistake. The theory used as ultimate propaganda for single-sex schools is that boys won't be around to distract the girls, and therefore they'll perform better. Ever been on a diet? When you're not near a bakery, you'll crave chocolate-glazed doughnuts even more! You can't take a few hundred teenage girls and lock them in a pretty white cashmere box for four years. They are hormonal, rebellious, and riddled with eating disorders.

I showed up at my chosen prep school, tucked away in the suburbs of New England, in colored patchwork corduroy pants and an electric pink sweater. I had my old camp trunk, a quilt, a pillow, and a Raggedy Ann doll with one eye. My dorm room was small, with two beds, two desks, and a bathroom down the hall for everyone to share. I tacked up my poster of a kitten clinging to a branch with the words "Hang in There!" in rainbow-shaped script above the kitten's head. My mother helped me make my bed and set up a five-dollar metal desk lamp. And then we were done. I was waiting for her to say, "This is depressing, a huge mistake, let's pack up and get the hell out of here."

She cleared her throat. "Well, I should get moving. I'm going to have dinner with Pebbles in Cambridge." I felt an ache in my chest, and my palms started sweating. (This was the first of a few panic attacks I would experience in my life.) I begged, pleaded, and cried for her to stay. As my mother pulled the Volvo out of the parking lot, I was hanging on to the front bumper, my sickly arms wrapped around the chrome appendage, my feet braced in the gravel. Either I would stay in that position while we traveled home, or my mother would have mercy somewhere on the Mass. Pike and let me in the passenger side.

It had been two hours since my mother peeled out of the school driveway when my roommate, Lucy, walked in with her father. She had a jolly smile, a plump face, and a nervous giggle. She and her father were from northern New Hampshire and had accents straight out of *Good Will Hunting*. Lucy's dad put down her suitcases, shook my hand, gave her a pat on the back—"Ah-rite Lucy, I gutta git bick in the cah before it gits too dahk"—and disappeared.

We walked together across the soccer field to the dining hall. It was unspoken but clear that whether we ended up liking each other or not, we were an army of two when we walked into the commissary. We would sit together, walk together, and act closer than we actually were. Your first friend at boarding school, camp, or prison is your life raft, and you always have each other's back. Luckily Lucy and I genuinely liked each other, which made the first few months tolerable. If I had ended up with one of the Asian girls in our class who always got awards and went to MIT early decision, I never would have been able to keep up, although I'd know how to rock a Hello Kitty minidress, and I'd probably own half of China!

⁂

I realized quickly that in boarding school the only method of survival was to smoke. Like in prison, if you have cigarettes you're exalted and safeguarded. There was one room designated for smokers, which was elegantly named the "butt room." One had to walk through it to enter the end of the dorm closest to the main classroom building. So in bad weather, if you didn't smoke, the walk from one end of the rancid basement strewn with filters and ash to the other was excruciating. You could almost hear, "Dead man walking!" So I learned how to smoke cigarettes. Like most urban gangstas, I chose Kool menthols as my brand, eventually switching to Virginia Slims Menthol Lights. I mean, I was a lady, for God's sake. I remember endless frigid nights spent sitting in the butt room under the fluorescent lights in our Lanz nightgowns, puffing away as we debated virginity—who had it and who didn't.

Around Thanksgiving was when the landscape changed. The trees were barren, every day was gray, and sports practices took place in the dark. It was this time of year that girls, no matter how much they smoked, started to succumb to the doldrums of winter and the environmental depression it brings. Everyone would order pizza nightly to ensure that each day would have a silver lining. The same way a recently married friend of mine told me, "The way I get through sex with my husband is I close my eyes and visualize the Oreo I'm going to treat myself to when it's over." In those days pizza and carbs were a teenage girl's antidepressants. When the tattooed pizza guy finally showed up with the boxes, the girls would swarm him (testosterone and pepperoni? Be still my heart!), and the trust fund babies would shell out an enormous tip. After pizza I would fall asleep to the sounds of my neighbor forcing herself to throw up down the hall. She was from Tallahassee, where it's imperative to be skinny and tan all year round. From what I understand, she runs the Orlando Hooters now.

It was around this time that Lucy started spending more and more time in the infirmary, a building with six rooms, painted a variety of repulsive pastel colors like crème de menthe and eggnog, with two iron beds in each. I don't remember being sick there, just faking it to get some extra sleep. All I wanted to do was eat cheese out of a can and sleep sixteen hours a day. The nurse always gave us pills, lots of (sugar) pills. I would take them with ginger ale and slide into a coma. And that was as close to a break as I got for four years.

I never knew what exactly Lucy was sick with.

Whenever she came back, she had no discernible symptoms; she was just a bit pallid and less animated. It was a Monday afternoon before Christmas vacation when the ambulance pulled up in front of the dorm. I was walking back from art class and saw two technicians get out and greet the headmistress. Then everyone walked somberly into the building. I was told to wait downstairs. I sat quietly on the mustard-colored sofa in the waiting area. Usually this space was used for storing lacrosse sticks or collecting mail. I had never actually been stationary in the room before. I looked up to see white shoes descending the stairs backward, then some Keds flailing, and then another pair of white sneakers. It was Lucy. She had a white canvas straitjacket tied around her middle, and she was thrashing like a marlin begging to be thrown back. She was placed in the ambulance, and then, in the blink of an eye, it drove away. I sat on the sofa and watched the sky turn a deep aubergine. Dusk seemed to close the curtains on the event. Nothing had to be explained to me; I knew everything was different.

I got permission to visit Lucy twice at McLean Hospital. She was always simultaneously crying and smiling while chain-smoking. I got the impression she didn't know where she was or what had happened, so I kept our conversations to simple categories like field hockey scores and who had cheated on their midterms. I would sit on her roommate's bed across from her and nod and smile and try not to run screaming though the glass security doors. She kept repeating, "We can smoke in here, so that's good, no butt room!" and she'd stamp out another cigarette into a makeshift aluminum foil ashtray. After the second visit I never went back. The thing about mental hospitals is—they make you feel crazy!

———— ⌘ ————

I never got a new roommate that year; I think the school felt I could use the mending period before assigning me another unstable adolescent. I did befriend two other girls who were on my floor. There was Della, a former toddler pageant winner from Atlanta, and Lulu, a hippie from Marin County, California. Bella had plastered the whole wall with magazine cutouts of beautiful clothed and unclothed models. It looked like the creepy inner sanctum of a serial killer, minus the newspaper clippings circled in red lipstick. But a shrine to obsession nonetheless.

Every night Bella would lay out her outfit for the next day, down to the hair clip, belt, earrings, and lip gloss shade. I found this extraordinary, considering most girls wore their pajamas to class, or the nearest thing they could pull off the floor. She even had a skin regimen, a nighttime ritual that involved five different jars. This was my introduction to astringents and exfoliators. Sea Breeze and a cotton ball were no longer sufficient; apparently my skin was in desperate need of cleansers found only on the first floor of Neiman Marcus. If there was a feminine component missing in my education, I had found it in the shape of a petite Georgian who owned an elaborate manicure set and used a safety pin to separate each lash after applying mascara. She taught me to wear earth tones, big belts, and brow highlighter. She ate cottage cheese and lettuce every day for lunch, and whenever I had a bowl of Sugar Pops with whole milk, she would look at me with such disappointment that I felt like a puppy who had just disemboweled the couch. There were moments when I got tremendous pleasure out of torturing her with raw cookie dough during all-nighters. I may have been twenty pounds heavier, with overgrown brows, but I much preferred watching her do sit-ups from the sideline with a box of Entenmanns's Brownie Chunks. It is my firm belief that if Bella had eaten Halloween candy and Rice Krispies Treats back then, she wouldn't be spending Saturday nights on a StairMaster tagging articles about surrogates and anal bleach kits today.

Lulu did not possess Bella's svelte figure or discipline; she was the opposite. Lulu was voluptuous, with heaving breasts and a thick mane of orange ringlets. She dressed and looked like a carrot-top, Shakespearean Janis Joplin dipped in freckles. My introduction to Lulu took place in the middle of the night. I was asleep. She snuck into my room, shook my shoulder, and asked if she could talk to me.

"Sure," I whispered, wondering how I could possibly be of any help to her. She was groovy, drank blackberry wine, and wore a floppy felt hat.

"Well," she whispered back, "Would you come with me to Boston this weekend to get an abortion?"

I had no idea what an abortion was. It was not something that came up at Girl Scouts. "Of course," I answered. "I'll get one too." (Thank God hers was a false alarm. Otherwise I'd probably be missing my pancreas.)

Lulu was the first and only nymphomaniac I have ever known. If Oprah did a show on sex addiction, it would be Lulu, Charlie Sheen, and a whole bunch of football players on the couch. At night Lulu would sneak out of the second-floor window and, like a cat in heat, promenade into town, a sleepy New England village that shut down at 6:00 p.m. There were no bars or clubs, but she would trawl the streets like a vampire searching for fresh blood. She would meet a cop having his cup of joe or a townie listening to Black Sabbath in his Camaro—the details weren't relevant. They'd have nameless, faceless sex, and afterward she would just crawl back through the window before dawn with pink cheeks and a wicked smile on her face. I can only imagine her Facebook page today (lots of people to befriend)! During a particular heavy patch or full moon, Lulu would have to go to the infirmary for a day to recover; she needed pills, sleep, and a bag of frozen peas. And then there were the nights she couldn't escape, when the dorm mother was patrolling the halls like a prison warden or campus security was parked out front. Lulu would dance around the room completely naked like a psychedelic wood nymph. She would blare the Rolling Stones or Pink Floyd until she worked herself up into such a state she would collapse, covered in sweat. I assumed that was how witches masturbated.

And there was the group of girls that were untouchable. You had to be either a junior or a senior even to be eligible to run with that pack. You also had to smoke, dress in ripped jeans that partially exposed your underwear (ghetto for debutantes), and have rope bracelets stacked up your arm. It was required you be obsessed with the Grateful Dead and have a summer home in either Nantucket or Martha's Vineyard. Renters didn't count unless you were from Bermuda. One night I found myself in the butt room with this social hive of queen bees. And on my third cigarette I was invited into the conversation. Did I know where they could score some pot? That was their opener. I had to be very careful framing my response; my answer could jeopardize the next three years of my life. I had never smoked pot, let alone knew where to score some. "I'm out," I blurted, "just smoked the last batch." I prayed they came in batches and not blocks.

One of the girls knew a guy at Deerfield Academy, the Krispy Kreme of boys' schools, who was a

dealer. She went to call him and figure out the logis-
tics. "We should get some munchies." I stayed silent;
I assumed munchies were short drug lords. And then
the recruitment began. After swearing their Sicilian
code of silence, my ultimate trial was to go to IHOP
and get snacks for "the family." I would be accompa-
nying a senior named Suzanne who looked like Joan
Jett—same haircut, same scowl. I was still in my Lanz
nightgown and moccasin slippers when we snuck out
of the dorm and disappeared into the trees. I figured
we would get to know each other on the walk, tell
funny stories, and bond like we would at a sleepaway
camp. But when we reached Route 128, Suzanne held
out her thumb. All I could see in the flash of speeding
headlights was my mother's disappointed face. ("What
the hell are you doing? Wearing your pajamas outside
in the middle of the night?") The evening had taken
a dark turn.

A rusty Buick pulled over to the side of the road,
and as Suzanne sprinted toward it, I followed like a
needy little sister. She jumped into the front seat and
pulled me next to her. The driver was a bearded man
in his late twenties (think Jim Morrison in his tubby
years). His ashtray was overflowing with cigarette
butts, and the car reeked of B.O. and beer.

The driver swerved back and forth over the middle
grid as he asked perfunctory questions about who we
were and where we were from. Suzanne answered
like a pro; we were EMT nurses leaving our night

shift. The driver didn't seem to question the fact that Suzanne was in a lacy nightgown, fluffy robe, and leg warmers. But he didn't strike me as someone who knew what EMT stood for anyway.

All I remember is the car flipping over, not monster truck–show style, but fluid and in slow motion. The driver had swerved to avoid the side of a bridge. Next thing I knew my face was pressed against the soft roof. We sat there for what felt like hours. Finally I crawled out, pulling Suzanne with me, and ripping my nightgown on a jagged piece of rusty metal above the tire. When I looked at the car, it resembled a tin cockroach on its back. Stumbling backward from the wreckage, we heard from inside the Buick, "Holy shit!" followed by fits of laughter. Yes, kind sir, Holy shit.

We ran back to the dorm without stopping, talking, or catching our breath. I panted in my bed most of the night and had never felt so relieved to be on my bumpy mattress, alone in my dorm room. Why couldn't I have stayed in bed with my Raggedy Ann and *Scarlet Letter* CliffsNotes like everybody else?

CHAPTER SIX

hugs not drugs

There are good drunks, and there are bad drunks. I wouldn't say I was a bad drunk—I'm fun, I'd take my top off—I'm just a bad drinker. I physically cannot chug. I'm a sipper. And I inherited a very low tolerance to alcohol from my mother. She once drank a glass of white wine and performed the entire second act of *The Pirates of Penzance* in our kitchen. To a standing ovation. For me, one glass of white wine and I wake up in a Hyatt with a group of Persian businessmen.

Drinking was a big part of prep school—at least, it was at mine. I didn't like the taste of booze and dreaded the post–spring-break ritual of gulping the mini liquor bottles stolen off the plane. Sometimes I pretended to glug and faked drunk; I became very good at faking. A couple of years ago I was dirty dancing at a friend's Labor Day party. I was provocative and flamboyant as I jumped on the shoulders of my equally flamboyant and openly gay dance partner and had him mop me all over the floor. The next day a woman asked my friend, the hostess, Who was the crazy drunk on the dance floor? I consumed two ginger ales that night.

It wasn't easy charting the social waters of prep school. There was your compulsive liar, Scarlett, who told everyone she was the heir to the Tiffany and Co. fortune. Anyone who refers to Tiffany's as "Tiffany's and Co" is probably not the beneficiary of all that is inside those robin's-egg-blue boxes. She also claimed to be the daughter of J. Paul Getty and Diana Ross. Were they ever together? And my favorite—she shot her father for having a bastard out of wedlock, and her mother took the rap for her and fled to France. Needless to say, Scarlett had never heard of public records. And then there was the latent lesbian who always wanted to brush people's hair and could tell fortunes by reading belly buttons. And as always, your standard psychotic.

I met Karen when we were sophomores. She was a jock from Chatham, Mass.; cute, with a button nose and a smattering of freckles. We didn't have much in common; I couldn't sink a three-pointer if my life depended on it, and the idea of drinking rum and Cokes in a rowboat all night (the East Coasters' version of cow-tipping) was about as exciting to me as waiting in line at the DMV. But we tolerated each other for the sake of social sustainability. One weekend Karen invited me to spend the weekend at her house in Cape Cod. I was always desperate to leave school, the way a turtle scrambles for footing on the glass side of his terrarium, so I accepted. I imagined clambakes and round-robin tennis with her family; after all, she had a sister named Beetle. Her parents seemed nice enough, for elitist drunks who drove around in golf carts in Gilligan hats.

Friday night Karen's parents were going to a pot-luck, Beetle to a school dance, and her brother Archer to a lacrosse championship. Karen decided to invite some local boys she had grown up with over to the house; she had a crush on one of them (the one who could have been her brother's twin, gross). I was hoping for a movie and a few pints of Mint Oreo ice cream, but figured I could delay all that until after the boys left. They were what I expected—gray U. Mass hoodie sweatshirts, braces, and nonstop talk about where to find some beer (pronounced "be-ah"). They drank room-temperature Bud Lights while I perused her mom's *Architectural Digest*. I would insert a comment now and again just to keep myself awake. One of the boys, Skip or Scooter, kept asking me why I didn't want a be-ah. "AA," I nonchalantly answered. It shut him up.

And then, without warning, Karen snapped. "Why are you all over him?" she screamed at me. I looked up from the magazine. "Huh?" She had walked around the counter into the kitchen. "You're a slut! And I'm going to kill you!" I froze and prayed the little bout of crazy would pass quickly, or the beer buzz would kick in. Karen pulled the spray hose out from the sink and pointed it at me like it was a gun. "You try, you just try to take him, you bitch!" And then she pulled the trigger. I was soaked in water and disbelief. The boys got the hell out of Dodge, taking the rest of the be-ah and a bottle of bourbon from the liquor cabinet while I went to change my clothes.

I was left alone with a drunk lunatic somewhere near Bucks Creek marshes. I could either swim across the Atlantic toward Nantucket in the hopes of hitching a ride on an oil tanker, or risk hiding in the laundry room until dawn. I went to Karen's room, which was covered in Nadia Comaneci clippings and basketball medals, to find my knapsack of clothes. As I pulled off my wet shirt, I noticed a stack of music books on her desk; the covers were completely covered in scribbles. I took a closer look. (Cue the horror-film sound track.) Scrawled all over these books was my name. My name written in script, block letters, graffiti style, slanted to the right, slanted to the left, with hearts, with stars, my name WRITTEN OVER AND OVER HUN-DREDS OF TIMES! I tried not to throw up as I de-bated whether to call the Greyhound bus terminal or the police. I snuck out of the house, assuming Karen was in the garage looking for an ax, got to a local inn called Ye Olde something, and called a cab.

Back at the dorm that night, I dashed off a thank-you note to Karen's parents on my Crane stationery, explaining how I had forgotten about a geometry test and, being a high achiever, needed to get back and study. And thank them for the Bloody Marys. I couldn't write what I really wanted to: "Dear Mr. and Mrs. You Need Betty Ford, thank you for a surreal stay at your house of dysfunction and key parties! Your daughter needs shock therapy, and I feel like she may gun down some innocent bystanders in an Arby's one day if she isn't locked up. And I was so grateful not to be a victim of one of those jocks heading towards Riker's after he commits a series of preppy murders. Again thank you and sorry I couldn't stay for the full night of horrors, but I have some self-preservation and knew my life wouldn't end at the hand of a disturbed lesbian psychopath. See you at the book fair! Love, someone who will forever avoid you." Karen and I never discussed that night, nor was I ever alone with her again. Every once in awhile when I'm watching *20/20*, I keep thinking she'll turn up in a segment.

One of the many invaluable lessons I learned from preparatory school was that psychopaths come in all shapes and sizes. Abigail was an anemic blonde from Winnetka, Illinois. Abigail was light on the outside, but dark on the inside. She had a face like a fetus and wore Fair Isle sweaters, knee socks, and clogs. I met her in the library, where she was passing around a can of Sprite to random people. "There's something wrong with this soda, try it," she offered. Finally a Pakistani girl, who was just thrilled someone had spoken to her, took a sip. She examined the can and took another sip. "It's bad," she said, wiping her hand across her pierced mouth, and handed it back to Abigail. Abigail smiled, threw the can in the garbage, and walked back to the spot on the floor where she'd been trying to carve her initials into the side of a mahogany bookcase.

"What was wrong with the Sprite?" I inquired.

Without missing a beat, she looked straight at me and said nonchalantly, "Nothing, I just peed in it."

Abigail was sent to boarding school to try to exorcise the Lizzie Borden out of her. She was an albino Wednesday Addams who had no boundaries when it came to mischief and chicanery. You know, the kind of girl who was to blame when cutlery went missing? Shortly after we met, Abigail asked me if I wanted to walk into town to buy Doritos, the kind of jaunt that constituted the pathetic highlight of my adolescent imprisoned days. Abigail needed cash, so we stopped at the local bank. I sat by the window trying to spot other students who had made the trek to town for necessary sundries like tampons and low-fat cottage cheese. Suddenly an alarm went off, and two obese Irish guards converged on Abigail. I was escorted with her to the back room of the bank, where we were detained for four hours. I watched Abigail masterfully explain how she hadn't written the note that said, "Put all your cash into a large envelope and nobody will get hurt." She blinked her pale blue eyes. "Somebody must have already written it on the deposit slip. I just happened to pick it." Finally, we were allowed to leave without the bank calling the headmistress. We shared a bag of Cool Ranch Doritos on the way back to school, and with the corners of her mouth packed with bright orange crumbs she said, "I should have written 'I have a gun' instead of 'nobody will get hurt,' then that bitch wouldn't have hit the alarm."

Abigail always had cash in bricks, the way a gangster does in the movies, and it wasn't from a part-time job or allowance from her parents. She was a player always looking for game. Every time she flew back from Chicago she would take only her backpack, which she would check. Then at baggage claim she'd pull off the tag and act as though the backpack was her carry-on. She would then complain to passenger services that they'd lost her bag. She would be compensated for her lost Nikon camera, diamond earrings, and couture dresses. She scammed every airline, and by the end of junior year she could have bought a fleet of private jets.

Abigail would have been better served by joining a satanic cult or the Israeli army, but instead decided to fraternize with some of the girls from South America. There's only one thing Abigail was conspiring to get from Valeria and Blanca, who traveled from Boston to Cochabamba on long weekends, and it wasn't a command of the Spanish language. Blanca's father had bought her an apartment in Chestnut Hill so she would have a place to go when the rigors of academic life got to her and she felt "*loca* in her *cabeza*." She could practice her math at the Framingham mall with her platinum American Express and work on her physics by measuring grams of uncut cocaine.

Abigail invited me to go with her to Blanca's Scarface condo one weekend. Again, I never needed an excuse to feel unfettered and alive. So Abigail had one of her many outside friends call and pretend to be her Aunt Boots, inviting us to her home in Cambridge for a chance to see the Krokodiloes, Harvard's premiere a cappella group. Blanca had a cinnamon red Mustang stashed in a garage in Dedham. So we didn't have to ride the T, Boston's subway, which was riddled with pale college students who looked like vampires and unkempt older men in ratty tweed jackets who once believed they were a shoo-in for a Pulitzer, only to end up teaching at Bunker Hill Community College.

The apartment was mauve and nondescript. A king bed in the master, a stained cream-colored pleather sofa, a glass coffee table and huge TV in the living room, and a banana tree. There were no utensils in the kitchen or toilet paper in the bathroom. But there was a large ziplock bag of blow tossed on the Formica counter. There was no ritual involved; most of the time Blanca would be on the phone, screaming in Spanish to one of her many lovers south of the equator, as she dumped the snow on the table, cut, lined, and snorted. Abigail did the same while rapidly underlining our American history textbook with a yellow highlighter and screaming about how the Hitler Youth were just promoting nationalism and didn't deserve the bad rap.

I had never tried drugs, not even allergy medication. All I knew was Diet Coke made me shake, and excessive amounts of chocolate made me weep. I have always preferred to be lucid in life. My fear with drugs has always been that I'll eat the brownie laced with LSD and drive into the ocean. On a bicycle. And drown. Very slowly. I don't even take Sudafed for fear I'd have a bad reaction and stab an ex-therapist.

The only time I experimented with marijuana was right before a dinner party at the Porcellian Club at Harvard. My boyfriend Josh was a student there and was desperate to be admitted into the antediluvian establishment. Josh's roommate was one of those math geniuses who was always stoned. He was heavy, bearded, and seemed to only own one T-shirt, which read, "You are here," with an arrow pointing to a dot in the solar system. I think the dude ended up ruling Silicon Valley. As I sat awkwardly on Josh's bed while he showered, the roommate (sporting corduroys covered in bong water) handed me a joint. I only took two drags, but that was enough to make me believe I had permanently morphed into Bob Dylan. Everything I looked at was seen through a kaleidoscope lens, like in those films when people are laughing maniacally and their faces are out of focus and swirling around in a prism sequence. At the club's black-tie dinner, I opted not to speak, a strategy that would serve me well at future social events like the White House Easter egg roll. The waiters placed a large red snapper on the table, and for the rest of the night I was convinced the fish was staring at me. And sending me telepathic messages, like "Help." When the fish head was severed with a silver poisson cutter and its body filleted in half, I fainted. Lay Lady Lay, Lay across that big lace table.

That was the extent of my drug repertoire up to that point. So Abigail and Blanca, dressed like Miami hookers in Spandex jumpsuits, went off to a Euro-trash disco club to dance off the speed the coke was cut with. I passed on the prospect of being molested by a group of Polish car salesmen. Instead, I chose cable TV.

I lay on the leather—ah, pleather—sofa and watched the film *Mannequin* twice, imagining how amazing it would be to have a body made out of plastic. Much like Hollywood today. Blanca had said as she pulled on her red cowboy boots, "Mira, if ju want some Coca, ees okay." I held the baggie up to the light, bounced it on my knee, and shifted the mountain of white snow from one side to the other. It was two in the morning, and I was bored. I tapped a spoonful onto the glass table. I'd spent my life blowing things out of my nose and it seemed against nature to snort in a foreign substance. I tried a little, but felt nothing but a medicinal drip in the back of my throat. So I snorted more and more. I snorted nose candy throughout the entire movie *Valley Girl* (for which Nicolas Cage should have been nominated for an Academy Award, in my opinion).

When I got up to pee, the room started to whirl. I made my way to the bathroom like I was on a speed-boat driven by Daniel Craig. I threw up white liquid that resembled a paste used for découpaging tables. My hands were shaking, and clearly someone had thrown a grenade into my brain. I made what I considered a wise choice at the time: to immediately fly home to D.C. Something was wrong, my sensors were out of whack, and I needed balance, I needed my mom. I grabbed my clothes, books, and the bag of cocaine. My thinking was that I needed to come down slowly, so I'd taper off little by little. (What did I know? I wasn't raised in Coconut Grove!) I left the South American drug cartel and Abigail a note—"Freaked out, going home, thanks for the hospitality, you're out of Coke—Ali."

By the time the taxi pulled up at Logan airport, I was sweating profusely; a heart attack was imminent. And then, in slow motion, I saw guards and United Airline representatives eyeing me suspiciously. Everyone knew, and it was just a matter of time before I was surrounded by machine guns, blinding flood-lights, and salivating German shepherds. I ran to the ladies' room and flushed the white horse down the toilet. I was not going to spend my life in a Turkish prison!

The plane ride was endless. The stewardess looked concerned, kept asking me if I was okay and if I needed water. I was licking my lips like a puppy who'd been fed peanut butter.

My older brother, John, answered the front door. He was home from Brown for a few days. "What happened to you?"

I fell to the ground in the fetal position. "I snorted fourteen grams of cocaine!" This was not something he expected from me. He reacted with a combination of horror and pride. He called the cocaine hotline and had a long discussion with an ex-addict named Nancy who begged my brother not to give me any other substances. "She's tweaking from the crap it's cut with, not the actual cocaine itself. She should only drink water and eat steamed vegetables for the next few days." Are you telling me John DeLorean got through detox on bok choy?

I tossed and turned in my bed, moaning as my brother placed cold washcloths on my head. And then we heard the front door slam and our miniature dachshund, Chester, yelping. We knew. Muffie was home.

"She has the flu, so the school sent her home." My brother intercepted Mom as she cautiously entered my bedroom.

"They never called me? If she's sick, why did they make her travel?"

John was quick. "They wanted her to see the doctor here." Well, that made no sense, and the last thing you want to do when you're strung out on illicit drugs is be prodded by a medical professional and given a blood test.

My mother came over and felt my forehead. "She's cold!" She pulled the goose-down duvet up to my chin. Apparently, hyperthermia is a symptom of an overdose. That, or I was already dead.

My mother immediately took charge. She insists on antibiotics at the first nose drip. When she's sick, her side table is spilling over with bottles and Kleenex boxes, potions and remedies. Sleeping pills were placed in our mouths like the body of Christ when we were home for school breaks. They were to help us catch up on our sleep, even though that's all we did anyway.

She walked into my bathroom and inspected my medicine cabinet. She gingerly rearranged the contents, removing a bottle of Nyquil, some Tylenol, and something that's been recalled by now. "Here we go!" She extracted a prescription vial that had sat in the medicine cabinet since I had my tonsils out at twelve. She held it up to the light and smiled. "Amoxicillin will knock out any virus."

A mother's power is hypnotic. I offered not a whisper of protest as she lovingly fed me pill after pill, shot of Nyquil after shot of Nyquil. I knew the dangers of administering even more drugs to my toxic body, but

I was willing to play Sunny von Bülow if only to be cuddled and coddled that day, far from the rat race of defective teens.

And for my daughters reading this: I experimented with cocaine just once so you won't have to. By the time you're reading this I will have already shown you an unlimited number of drug documentaries, HBO's *Addiction, Celebrity Rehab, Heroin: The Next Generation, Intervention,* photos of drug-related overdose autopsies and the film *Valley of the Dolls.* I will have stamped out any need for experimentation (not to mention my photographic scientific textbook on sexually transmitted diseases). Besides, knitting is so much more fun!

mi familia!

As kids, we were shipped off more times than a Pottery Barn catalog. I had sleepaway camp at nine, boarding school at thirteen, and then Spain the summer of my fifteenth year. It was called "the experiment in international living." Disconcerting title, I know. Like they just parachute you down in Kazakhstan and see what happens. Well, actually, they kind of do.

I packed what any sheltered preppy in high school would when setting off for a European tour: seven Laura Ashley skirts, Bloomingdale's days-of-the-week undies, a tennis racquet, and my collection of Bonne Bell lip smackers.

I found myself standing in the Madrid airport with a group of gum-smacking teenagers in a sea of monogrammed L.L.Bean tote bags, lacrosse sticks, and duffels with old claim tickets from St. Kitts and Vail. I scrutinized the crowd and, as if picking out the least-expired lettuce from the salad bar, chose a girl named Jennifer to be my summer friend. Jennifer had long, chestnut-colored hair, eyes that looked perpetually stoned (because they were), a Rolling Stones tour T-shirt, dolphin shorts, tube socks, and Dr. Scholl's. She was never without a Walkman blaring from her ears. Even when we had our most private conversations, I could hear the dull roar of classic rock. Sometimes I couldn't tell if she was giving me genuine advice or just regurgitating the lyrics assaulting her at that moment. I mean, why would I want to fly like an eagle?

Lucky for us, we were both placed in the same town five hours outside Madrid, a desolate desert town called Zamora. I couldn't wait to charge Arnold Palmers at the beach club, shop for souvenirs, and meet a sun-kissed Spanish surfer (even though we were hundreds of miles from water). I even brought tubes of Clinique's fake tan mousse to jump-start my Mediterranean glow.

The bus we took to Zamora resembled the vintage transports that run through San Francisco's Chinatown. The majority of passengers were local farmers with—this is the truth—chickens and goats occupying seats next to them. The ride was cacophonous, turbulent, and stank like an unattended hamster cage. One woman, somewhere in her late nineties, wearing a scarf that had survived eight wars, stared at my Prince tennis racquet the entire trip. I figured she was thinking she could strain her rice with it. Or finish off that no-good husband.

Zamora looked like the back lot at Universal Studios where they shot the westerns starring Lee Marvin that run on unheard-of cable channels at odd hours of the night. While I gathered my personalized duffels, Jennifer flipped the Pink Floyd tape in her Walkman and added a new piece of Big Red gum to the wad in her mouth, and we both, with intense trepidation, began our perilous summer teen tour. There were two families standing across the road, anxiously trying to get a glimpse of the kid they were getting paid $200 a week to house. A fair exchange of "take my hormonal teen for the summer and you'll get a new cart for your donkey."

Jennifer's family seemed pleased when they met her, stroking her hair for an unhealthy length of time. We found out later that the last summer guest they had lodged was a boy from Paramus who wanted a homosexual experiment in international living. He chased their teenage son, Jesus, incessantly around the house and through the fields until Boy George was shipped back to New Jersey. Jesus now spends a lot of time in church.

My family was a jolly (read: obese) bunch who looked like a photo stretched to panaromic view. There was Papa, who looked like Javier Bardem if Javier Bardem had swallowed Penelope Cruz; Mama, a Hispanic Delta Burke (post–*Designing Women*); Jose (Spain's version of Charlie Brown); and three older sisters, who reminded me of increasingly chubby babushka nesting dolls.

I looked around for the Buick Regal or Chrysler

LeBaron, but before I knew it we were hoofing it up a hill, my suitcase and racquet dragged behind us by an extremely sweaty Jose. The house was a small three-bedroom they had built by hand with the help of the entire town—about fifty people, give or take a goat. It had a mud-and-straw-patched roof and looked like an *Elle Décor* photo of how I picture Michael Douglas's guesthouse in Mallorca, rustic and authentic. My room was quaint and cozy: a single bed with lumpy, lopsided hay-filled pillows and torn coverlet. A cross with an unhappy Christ nailed to it hung on the wall.

Dinner was like an all-you-can-eat Vegas buffet. There were potatoes baked in fat. Meat baked in fat. Fat baked in fat. After every third bite my Spanish father would hold up a goatskin sack and pour sangria down my throat. Then another course would come out, and another . . . I stumbled from the table, barely making my way to my bed; going up the stairs was like walking up a slide lined with Crisco. I collapsed, only to be awakened a few hours later for dinner. The earlier feast had been supper, not dinner. Like having breakfast, then immediately brunch. The Spaniards eat four meals a day. You know how geese are force-fed until their liver explodes to make foie gras terrine? I could barely keep my eyes open as the father poured another liter of sangria down my throat.

The next morning I woke up with what I thought was double vision from a throbbing hangover. I hallucinated a Spanish rave of people in my bed. And when I rolled over to stop the pain and got my right eye to focus, I realized this was, in fact, the case. I was in a bed full of Spanish people. Contrary to my assumption that I'd have an ounce of privacy, I did not have my own room; I shared it with Jose and the three gaseous sisters. To this day, when my husband accidentally touches me during the night, I sit up and scream, "Dios me ayuda!" (God help me!)

⸻ ✿ ⸻

The highlight of each week in Zamora took place on Wednesday, when the whole town would come over to our house at nine o'clock in the evening. My Spanish family had the only television in southern Spain, and Wednesday night was *Dallas* night. The talk of the stall mucking was what nasty thing J. R. Ewing (pronounced Hera Arra Oowing) was up to. The fifty townspeople would cram into the living room, saddling one another, to get a glimpse of the fourteen-inch black-and-white TV. There would be deafening silence until Linda Gray (whose voice was dubbed by a Hispanic male wrestler) screamed an ultimatum at the stable boy. The room would shake their heads with gasps and *tsk*s. One great-great-great-grandmother would stand up and, shaking her fists, scream at the actors as if certain she was getting through to them. My favorite moment of the evening was when our dog, Carne, would excrete the most heinous fart imaginable, and my father, without turning to face the canine, would spray generic room deodorizer in the dog's direction. After a childhood of black-tie dinners for the likes of Lady Bird Johnson, this was what I called a party!

It was during this summer that I learned that a pet could be your best friend and also your lunch. You could dress them in your doll's clothes and name them Buttercup or slaughter them over a bloody slab of stone out back. It was really a cultural choice.

Jose and I were playing our usual game—How many cookies can you cram in your mouth without choking?—when my mother waddled into the kitchen with a chore for me. "Yo necessito pollo por favor."

I knew she needed something, but *pollo* was drawing a blank. "Pollo," she repeated sternly.

"Like on horses? With a mallet?" We continued with this Abbott and Costello routine until finally Jose got up and starting clucking around the room. "Ohhh . . . chicken," I realized. "I'll go to the market," I assured her, using my fingers to mime the universal symbol of money. She and Jose looked at me with confusion. And then, like a Vegas bookie, I mimed counting money. She kept shaking her head. Perhaps I could just charge it to their account.

I walked down the parched road, choking on dust as I made my way into town. And by town, I mean one store of groceries and sundries the size of a New York kitchen run by a cantankerous old lady with no teeth (you know her as the lady who berates the people who live in the TV). I had gone about twenty-five yards when Jose, breathless, beckoned me back. I assumed my mother was adding to the list, maybe fruit roll-ups or coffee Häagen-Dazs. I, like my Spanish family, was now obsessed with all the gifts of the culinary world. I prayed for six meals a day; two hours between feedings felt like starvation and abuse, no matter how many lard balls and chocolate I ate to tide me over.

I slogged back up the road and followed Jose around the back of the house to an arid field. There was a chicken coop and loose (or as the Californians say, cage-free) hens chortling about. He pointed to one. "Uh-huh," I said. "Is that your favorite?" He repeatedly pointed to the hen. "What? You want me to name it?" And then Jose made a gesture normally only associated with serial killers and Robert De Niro. He took his two palms and made a snapping noise while he turned them swiftly counterclockwise.

"KILL IT? Are you out of your fucking mind?" Jose chased the chicken around for ten minutes, occasionally slipping on bird turds, until he snagged it by its ruffled left wing. He placed it in my arms. I don't know if you've ever held a live chicken, but it's like holding a puppy after it's drunk ten espressos. Jose placed my hands around the chicken's neck and then had the audacity to smile. I tried to twist the neck, but it was more of a massage than a proper wrenching; the bird did seem to relax. Finally, Jose, who had reached the breaking point, so to speak, grabbed the chicken, bent it over his knee, and snapped the neck. As easily and swiftly as one would break twigs for kindling. The bird went limp and fell to the ground. I was right behind it.

I felt like Hannibal Lecter that night, sopping up the chicken stew with hunks of crusty bread. But I was starving; it had been forty-five minutes since my last meal. You'd think that afternoon massacre would have prompted a conversion to veganism, but one taste of the spicy sausage in the paella shackled my compassion. To this day I have repeated nightmares in which the souls of all of the animals I've eaten gather to gnaw me to death. Yet I always wake up with a yen for bacon.

———— ⟋⟍⟋ ————

I spent the rest of the summer cutting slits in the elastic waistbands of my skirts. I had gained thirty-five pounds, most of which went right to my face. It was as if someone had put a bicycle pump up my mouth and inflated until the brink of explosion. After almost three months of asking, "Quien disparo JR?" and scarfing *tortillas de patatas*, I decided to meet my best friend, Holly, in Paris before returning to the land of Ann Taylor, Skittles, and MTV. Holly was having her own teenage summer abroad, just more luxe. She lived with a French family on avenue Foch, in the chicest arrondissement of Paris. She was smoking Gitanes and being courted by French boys with silk ascots and tailored shirts. The only chicken she choked belonged to a French banker's son, in the garden maze of their weekend chateau.

We decided to travel to Brittany and stay in a bed-and-breakfast. It was the first time we had traveled unchaperoned; this was before AMBER Alerts, and children on milk cartons were just getting started. The notion of anything *Law & Order SVU* happening to us never crossed our minds, perhaps because we were more predator than prey. Today I am so paranoid, I tried to find a GPS-tracking chip to implant in my daughter's scalp so if she were ever abducted, I could track her down like a missing Honda. I still may buy the patent.

The first order of business in the majestic northeast part of France was to ignore the ravishing countryside with the misty moors, and lose pounds. We were both pudgy (read: fat), and needed to slim down before we went back to Paris, a city where women look like walking wind chimes with blunt haircuts and poppy red lipstick. So we created our own diet, a cleanse of sorts. We drank only black tea with heaps of sugar and triple cream. Take that, South Beach diet! After two days we became weak and light-headed insomniacs and back in Paris decided to trade in our weight-loss pact for a platter of profiteroles and that cheese at Café Lipp that smells like feet.

I didn't think it possible for me to tip the scales at 140 pounds, but when I arrived at Dulles International Airport, I was pushing 153 pounds. I had become the "before" in the Jenny Craig posters. As I collected my luggage at baggage claim (I had left the tennis racquet in Zamora; Jose begged to have it to play Hit the Cowpatty Over the House), I scanned the crowds. And then I spotted her. My mother was wheeling an airport cart in my direction. She was statuesque and tan and gracefully pushed the cart before her like a stewardess offering the warm cookies in first class.

I smiled. I was ecstatic to see her—and the Burger King sign just beyond. She got closer and closer. She smiled, I smiled; my steps turned to a light trot, my arms outstretched. And then . . . she walked right past me.

I paused for a Whopper and then set off to find her.

CHAPTER EIGHT

happy and preppy and bursting with love

Losing my virginity was about as romantic as a flu shot. The problem with having a sheltered and protected upbringing is, you're not prepared for anything alien and outlandish, like the penis. We never discussed sex at home. Everything I learned about sex was from deodorant commercials and slasher films. The lesson—if you were slutty you'd be the first bludgeoned.

In the summer of my sixteenth year, I was given the choice of going to sleepaway camp or getting a job. I felt I was too old for collecting patches based on my fire-starting skills and yet too young for any substantial employment like D.C. mayor or editor of the *Washington Post*. My mother offered me a job filing in her office, but I make it a point not to mix business with non-pleasure. I was sitting on the sofa of our Mark Hampton–designed blue-and-white chintz guest room, scraping out the middle of a gooey wheel of Brie, when I had a revelation. I thought to myself, "What are my summer goals?" Well, that was easy; I wanted money and fame. But what else? What was I passionate about? And then it hit me—chocolate. I love chocolate. It was that flicker of genius that led me to become the neighborhood Cake Boss.

I recruited my friend Christina to partner with me. Christina was basically sunbathing on the roof of her house all day, and this adventure saved her from atrophy, and probably skin cancer. The startup was easy. We would walk to the corner grocery where my mother had an account and charge eggs, flour, sugar, bittersweet chocolate bars, some sandwiches for lunch, a pint of coffee ice cream, and some Milk Duds. The fantastic thing about my business was that there was zero overhead, which put us ahead of the game before we sold our first cake. After quick pit stops at the Gap and 7-Eleven (for Big Gulps), we would make our way back to my house and begin our respective chores. I would mix and sift and bake while Christina made prank phone calls to boys she liked. And thus, much like the profitable and innovative Ben & Jerry's, a successful partnership was formed.

My mother has always been helpful in discreetly giving success a little pat on the rear. She began calling friends to advertise the fact that culinary masterpieces were being created in her own kitchen, and wouldn't they want to (have to) buy one? Within two weeks, I was knee-high in melted chocolate. There were so many calls coming in for cakes, Christina had to reduce her prank calls to no more than nine an hour. Luckily, there were soap operas. Just when we were teetering into confectionery doldrums, someone on *All My Children* would be raped and, like a shot of B12, it would give us enough energy to finish the orders for the day. We were even beginning to receive long-distance orders, the problem being that these cakes required shipping. My mother received lemon Bundt cakes in round reindeer tins every Christmas from a billionaire friend, but these were obsolete in the middle of June. I ended up buying cardboard moving boxes, dropping a cake in, duct-taping it shut, and marching it over to the post office. The socialites from Sacramento or Chicago were too polite to complain about a smashed box full of crumbs.

One sweltering August day Christina and I were invited to a make-out pool party, which resulted in Christina spending the whole workday spray-tanning her feet and holding a tray of tin foil under her face in the backyard. Meanwhile inside I was Durga, the Hindu goddess with eight arms, shoving pans in the oven and double-boiling chocolate chunks. We had one last delivery in the neighborhood, which I made solo while Christina headed to her house to mousse her hair and pick out a revealing blouse. All our deliveries were made on foot, so if the cake was not bound for somewhere within a ten-block radius, we had to beg one of our parents to drive us. The night of the party, the delivery was so close, I decided to just drop the cake off en route. After all, I wasn't that excited about the party; it would be the same old people, I can't drink tequila upside down, and I was exhausted. My hair was spackled with flour, and my blue-and-white-checked apron was Jackson Pollocked in chocolate.

And then he sauntered in. Chad was what every prep-school girl coveted. He was naturally blond and blue-eyed, with a body perfected by the St. Paul's crew team, Mick Jagger lips circa 1961, a sun-kissed face, and cheekbones you could slice a mango with. He wore frayed khakis and a faded vintage Harvard T-shirt. He was a genetic masterpiece. It was like the moment in *King Kong* when the villagers see the ape for the first time and all fall to the ground. "Ladies and Gentlemen, I give you Kong! The eighth wonder of the world!"

I have never been the girl in a wet T-shirt contest or the type who rides the bull in a bikini—quite the opposite. I approach my prey skillfully and discreetly, like a python sidling up to a mouse. The unshowered, unkempt look was not winning me any points in the swimsuit competition, however, so I relied on talent, which for the past few weeks had been reduced to measuring brown sugar and vanilla extract. Chad demonstrated little interest in me, which only made the pursuit that more challenging. I was about to throw in the dish towel when out of nowhere, Chad asked the room if anyone wanted to drive to Delaware Beach to catch the sunrise. The trip was three hours—each way. I threw my hand up. "What the hell, yeah! Let's do it!" Christina looked at me like I had just volunteered for the Navy SEALs. A couple of nondescript boarding-school friends and the disproportionately limbed kid who threw the party offered to ride with him. Chad had his own car, a Twizzler-red Honda. Swoon. Clearly, there was no room for me. I had to act fast. "It's cool, I'll drive. I have my own car."

My mother's VW Rabbit was parked in front of our townhouse. There was just one microscopic wrinkle. I didn't have a driver's license, a detail that failed to deter me. I was given ten minutes to run home, rip off the apron, spray in my Psssssst instant shampoo, and get "my car."

I returned in madras shorts, a white button-down Talbot's Oxford, and espadrilles. I rambled up the driveway in the VW like I was driving Miss Daisy. My father had taken me to abandoned parking lots to practice driving, so I was adept at steering and turning. I didn't know any road rules, but could locate the horn and tape player, which I felt was good enough.

Chad and his friends sped down Route 95 blaring the Grateful Dead, their bare feet sticking out of the back windows. Desperate to keep up, I clenched the steering wheel with drenched palms, eyeing the right-hand emergency lane at all times. And under my breath I sang, "Jesus loves me, this I know, for the Bible tells me so."

We pulled up to the boardwalk parking lot just before sunrise. Chad was impressed that I had driven independently to the beach, sans gaggle of giggly, lip-gloss-applying girlfriends. Yeah, I was a lawbreaking, badass gangsta who rode alone!

The rest of the morning played out like a saccharine Oxygen channel movie. We walked on the sand, dipping our toes in the surf. We enchanted each other with our greatest hits—grade point average (okay, I lied), passion for table tennis, best fried clams in Maine, the usual banter. And then we kissed. I felt lipless as he pressed his glazed doughnut of a mouth on mine. First love uncoiled its dewy petals.

It was about two o'clock in the afternoon the next day when I pulled into the same parking space in front of our house. It had never entered my mind there would be consequences for my renegade behavior. I was a first-timer, no rap sheet. On the front door was the picture of a kennel and bone with a chain leading to a photo of me taped to it. I was in the doghouse?

Christina had broken under the inquisition. My

mother thought I was spending the night at her house, and when she called just to check in Christina started babbling, unprompted. "Hey Nazis, she's in the attic."

"You are grounded for the rest of the summer," my mother yelled, pointing her finger at me, in case I missed the object of her wrath.

"Okay." I sighed passively.

Unwittingly, I was squirting lighter fluid on the fire. "Not only are you grounded for the summer, but you will do all the dishes for every meal!" she yelled again.

"Got it," I whispered unresponsively.

"You are grounded for the summer, have to do the dishes and . . . no friends can come over. Ever!"

I cleared my mousy throat. "I understand."

My mother was shaking with constipated rage. "I have to go to New York this weekend, and you are coming with me!"

"No."

"Oh, yes, you are! I am not leaving you here alone. You are coming with me to New York!"

"No. I'm not going."

"You listen to me young lady, you are going with me to New York, do you understand?"

"Mom, you can't force me on the plane!"

She paced the living room and while checking the soil of an orchid announced, "Okay! New punishment! You're not grounded or have to do the dishes, but you have to come to New York with me this weekend!"

I fell to the ground as if touched by a televangelist before fleeing to my room, where I fake-sobbed loudly. How had I become such a genius? When you turn fugitive, is your criminal mind naturally sharpened? I should have been grounded for years! She should have taken away all my inalienable rights! But instead, my punishment was to accompany her to New York?

It was one of the best weekends I ever had. My mother and I shopped at Bergdorf's, dined at Swifty's, a WASP watering hole, and saw the musical *A Chorus Line*. And by Monday morning I was humming "Tits and Ass" on my way to meet Chad for pancakes.

The rest of the summer consisted of Beach Boy concerts, BBQs, and paddleboating on the Potomac. I know, sappy, but when you're in love you don't care, you'll change rattraps.

We parted in September, both of us flying north to our respected institutions of higher education. Chad's was a coed stone fortress perched on a snowy hill in New Hampshire, mine a Cape Cod shingled manor that housed a variety of girls behind bars. We wrote pages and pages of love letters, had the occasional pay phone conversation, and once in a while met in Boston. We would sleep on the foldout sofa in his brother's Harvard graduate housing complex in Cambridge. He would lie there and read Hemingway aloud while I strained not to fart.

It wasn't until Thanksgiving, when we were both back in D.C., that I decided the moment was ripe for his plucking.

His parents lived on a ramshackle farm in northern Virginia. Ramshackle not in the quaint Edith Wharton sense of the word but in the mice-infested, creepy *Shining* sense. Vines were growing through the walls; the roof leaked like a running faucet. Chad's mother never left the house, wore the same housecoat every day, and spoke to the animals like a Dr. Dolittle on mushrooms; there wasn't a cuckoo's nest she hadn't flown over. I liked her; she was loopy and nonsensical and was constantly asking me why I was wasting my time with her boy. One day Chad and I walked into the kitchen to find her frying hot dog buns. As we touched upon topics such as why one of the horses had jumped the fence into oncoming traffic, she would scrape the buns out of the pan, wrap them in tin foil, and place them in the freezer.

It was a frosty November night when we drove to the nearest 7-Eleven. Collectively, we knew very little about copulation. We browsed the candy section like it was a gallery in Chelsea; Chad bought some Starburst and casually asked for condoms. I almost ran through the plate-glass window. The word, the idea, the act—it was all enough to send me over the edge. "What size?" the corpulent woman with beady eyes asked. Come on! You don't ask a nervous seventeen-year-old boy that! He's not asking for socks! And frankly, I didn't want to hear the answer. "Plain or lubricated?" Now I was going to vomit. Maybe it would be easier to just make the condoms ourselves at home. I could sew!

Back at the farm we retreated to his room and read the back of the condom packet, poring over each step of the directions and every line of the warnings like a pair of *Scientific American* interns. I think we even memorized the ingredients, expiration date, and plant number: polyurethane, nonoxynol-9, June 1981, and DAO.

I'll spare you the details because, believe me, it won't read like a *Penthouse* letter. More like a Guantanamo confessional. It hurt. So much so that I'm surprised I ever got back on that horse again, if you know what I mean.

The next night Chad took me to dinner to celebrate our rite of passage. And to reassure ourselves that it was all okay because one day we would marry. We went to a French bistro that was known less for their escargots than for the fact that they delivered the food on roller skates. The restaurant is now defunct; too many lawsuits. We were dressed in clothes reserved for chapel and college interviews. I had just bitten into my endive salad when my vision began to blur and yellow stars began to swirl around the table like a *Starlight Express* acid trip.

The next thing I remember was waking up in a

hospital bed at Georgetown University Hospital. There was a gynecologist present, so naturally I assumed I had given birth. Chad was pale and shaky. He thought I had given birth, too. The doctor explained to us that pregnancy encompassed nine months, not two days, and that I had torn a tissue in my vagina, which had caused bleeding. Perhaps we should have bought Magnums after all?

A few weeks later I was skipping out the door to meet Chad for . . . ahem, let's just say miniature golf. I had almost closed the front door when my mother called me in to her office for a second. Whenever my mother called me in to her office, it was never for a second. We sat on the couch, and she studied me like an opposing prosecutor. "Are you okay?" she asked with concern.

"Um, yes."

"Anything you want to talk to me about?" She leaned in. I assumed she'd found the Chinese bowl I broke earlier that summer and stashed under my sister's bed. But before I launched into an elaborate lie pinning it on Sissy, my mother pulled out a pink print from her bag. "I got this bill from the emergency room." Damn health care system. I didn't know if or how I was covered, and so we had given the emergency room Chad's mother's credit card, along with my address.

We both sat in silence. And then my mother

smoothed her skirt. "And you're okay? The doctors said it's all fine?"

"Uh-huh."

"Well, that's good."

And then my mother said something to me that I have never forgotten and which made me feel so protected and connected to her. It was slightly over my head at the time, but I've carried it with me to this day. She looked directly in my eyes, "If you or your sisters ever find yourselves in trouble, you come to me! I don't need some jackass emptying out his piggy bank and taking you to some half-cocked, rundown clinic."

I never had to take her up on this. Although, I remember when my college boyfriend (holding chopsticks and a spatula) came flying into the room screaming, "Ill tell you if it's a cyst!"

tennis, anyone?

I was not a competitive child. I never experienced in-somnia when I half-assed a paper on John Adams or the origins of poison ivy. I didn't play team sports, and rose only to a mediocre level in skiing and tennis. These were the two sports our family trips were built around and, I was told, would benefit me socially when I was older. I never competed for boys, choosing instead to live by the motto, "If you love something, set it free, if it comes back to you, it's yours; if not, well, then he's an asshole." I did, however, compete for some attention. I was the youngest of the first marriage and middle of the extended family, so it was my psychological prerogative to scratch the door until I was noticed. My stepfather loved a party trick that involved picking me up by my jawbone until my little feet dangled off the floor. In the olden days they called it a hanging. But if that was what it took to get a little applause, I would always put my neck out. The payback was forcing him and my mother to sit through two hours of me lip-synching the entire *Free to Be . . . You and Me* album.

During the summers on the Cape my mother was an avid tennis player. The hair-sprayed Nancy Reagan coif and sparkling kaftans were ditched in D.C., exchanged for faded jeans, white JCPenney T-shirts, and tennis whites. Some days she would garden or go to the local farmer's market in her tennis whites and never actually make it to a court. Fashionistas would say it's the outfit that transitions into anything.

Most women wear their tennis skirts just above the knee, with some sort of sewn-in panty underneath. My daughters call them skorts. Or they were bloomers. My mother's skirt was significantly shorter, and she wore nothing underneath but her nylon underwear. She didn't care about the fashion, comfort, or perception; it was a white skirt, and that was what was required of a tennis ensemble. It was the same "Oh, who's really paying attention" attitude that would compel her to strip down to her Maidenform white bra and translucent underwear and dive into the ocean. While my siblings and I screamed in horror from the sand, she would shout back, "Oh, c'mon, it looks like a white bikini." Well, not when she emerged from the surf. If you were standing more than two feet away and couldn't detect the minuscule clips on the bra, she was stark raving naked. In the middle of a July afternoon. On a public beach. In Cape Cod.

And as Cape Cod was the mandatory destination for family time, I had to leave Chad's embrace and inflated lips for the month of August. When you're a teenager and you're separated from your soul mate du jour, a month is an eternity of Crosby, Stills and Nash songs and answering every phone call on the first ring. Chad's parents were in South Africa for the summer and left him with the house, the car, and a Visa card. The world was his oyster. And I, his pearl, was smoking cigarettes behind the local Tastee Freez. My days were unstructured: sleep, eat, beach, eat, sleep, eat (although the order could change, depending on the weather).

We were having one of our traditional lobster races one night. We would write numbers in nail polish on each of the lobsters' shells and then race them on the back porch. I know, PETA, I know, how could we torture them and boil them alive? Boredom. It was a stretch to call it a race; it was more of a death march. We once had a bracket of rambunctious lobsters that scurried around with so much vigor, we ended up losing one. My little sister had to share, and while everyone focused on the injustice of Fiona not getting both claws, I imagined how someday there would be thousands of spawned lobsters living under our house. And slowly moving the whole structure closer and closer to and then into the ocean.

As we watched our lifeless crustaceans try to muster up the energy to slither an inch, I asked my mother, "Mom, there's really nothing for me to do here . . . can I go back to D.C. to see my friends?"

"You mean Chad?" She raised that eyebrow.

"Yes, but also get ready for school . . ."

She gave me that look. "School doesn't start for a month."

I adjusted my lobster's broken antenna. "Why do I have to stay here? Why? What do I have to do to go home?"

"We are here for the month, that's it, end of discussion."

I pretended to concentrate on the amazing race. "What if I beat you in tennis?" The idea was ludicrous. I was a C+ player for my age group, always hitting balls into the other court and hurting players.

"Okay," said my mother, both eyebrows raised to their devil's peak.

I was startled. "You mean if I beat you in a set of tennis, you'll let me go back to D.C.?"

She graced me with a condescending smile. "Yes, if you beat me in tennis."

We walked down to the Eel River Beach Club the next morning and took one of the courts by the parking lot. We could hear the seagulls cawing as they rifled through the open Dumpster, one occasionally flying off with the tip of a hot dog roll in its beak. I wanted to dive right into the competition just like those flying rats, but my mother insisted we warm up. She was so polished, with her follow-through moves and slamming serves, her long tan legs dancing across the court. I was convinced my racquet was badly strung, as the majority of the balls I hit flew over the court fence, nearly hitting the gulls and causing a ruckus.

My mother collected three balls in her left hand. "You ready to start?"

I nodded.

To this day, I have never been as focused as I was that afternoon in Plymouth, Mass. I willed myself to be a better player than I was. I was nailing her lobs, smashing her net shots, and slicing my returns. I was Chris Evert without bangs. My mother grew serious; it was no longer fun and volleys, but a competition with the reality of something to lose. I played off her mistakes, which only seemed to multiply them.

It was match point; I was ahead by one game. The sun was beating down on us, a fat kid covered in blue popsicle juice was watching through the chain-link fence, and we could hear the loudspeaker by the pool: "Adult swim, everyone out of the pool except for seniors, it's adult swim. Hey Anthony—are you swimming without trunks?" It was my mother's serve. She bounced the ball about eight times before she flung it up into the air. It was wide. Again, she bounced the next ball about nine times. She tossed it, smacked it, and we both eyeballed it as it narrowly missed the baseline.

I won. I had beaten my mother in tennis. I broke into hysterical laughter. "I won! I won!" And then

I paused, preparing myself for the disappointment of my mother explaining to me that she had never been serious about the bet and how it was fun just to play.

As she started gathering up our tennis balls, though, she smiled. "I'll call the airline."

Game over!

london calling

In our family the concept of a purposeless summer was anathema. As a college girl I couldn't bear another session of tennis camp (most of the campers were nine) and didn't feel like being a mother's helper to some spoiled towhead on Fishers Island who spoke with a lisp and peed in golf bags. My mother suggested an internship. An internship, in her eyes, was a mind-enhancing experience, which would serve me well in future job applications. To me, an internship just meant I was working for no pay. The question was what and where. I was leaning toward concession stand operator in charge of Junior Mints or nail technician, but I knew I didn't want to live at home in the sweltering humidity of Washington, dining on endive salad and sorbet with my mother and stepfather every night. Plus, I didn't have a beauty school license. And, not being the outdoorsy type, anything in the Outward Bound arena like mountain-climbing leadership programs was out of the question. I wasn't going to skin and eat possum meat (without French dressing).

When my mother threatened me again with a job answering phones at her office, we compromised on an internship at Christie's, the art and auction house, in London. I was feeling very adventurous and Anglophilic. And I always have a hankering for clotted cream.

As I was counting down the hours until I could spread my wings, my mother pulled out her shears and clipped them. She insisted I stay with family friends. Poof went my fantasy of a swinging, Austin Powers–type flat, replaced by a room that boasted buttercup yellow curtains and a single bed on the top floor of a town house on St. James's Place. The mother and father were bankers, and the son was head of the debating society at Oxford. Not the types to roll joints and jump around in popsicle blue leisure suits all night, no way baby! Not that I wanted that; I just liked the idea of the option. The house was filled with oil paintings of stern-looking ancestors and yelping Jack Russell terriers. I expected Jane Austen to come flying in the parlor door at any minute with a basket of wildflowers, a stack of parchment love letters, and some serious boy trouble.

As much as I was infatuated with a British accent and fancied anyone who had one, I did have a boyfriend in the States at the time. Tim was from an unpronounceable town in the middle of Long Island. Hopapogue or Pagapougue. Anyway, Tim was a filmmaker. And a drinker. Well, he was Irish. Tim never passed on a pint of Guinness, and was jealous of my proximity to it. When I went to London for the summer, he acted like I was joining the Peace Corps (to him anywhere outside Long Island was on a different time zone and was festering in malaria), even though he had already taken a job at an Alaskan fish cannery. We communicated exclusively through letters, which, by the time I had received one, reported obsolete, weeks-old news. I would write to him about my strolls through the Tate Museum, the bucolic English countryside, and the exceptional interiors of the British Parliament. Tim would regale me with the fetid stench of fish guts, a dysentery outbreak, and how he contracted crabs from an old sleeping bag. I would sit on the benches of Hyde Park watching young lads in white linen play cricket and writing Tim pages and pages of poetry. He would mail me his toenail clippings. Love is blind.

The first day of my internship I was escorted up magnificent limestone stairs to the prints and watercolors department at Christie's. There I met my boss, Percy Talbot. He was a persnickety man in a finely tailored suit and tortoiseshell glasses who wore his black hair slicked to the side, and a fresh gardenia pinned to his lapel. He didn't make eye contact with me or shake my hand. Instead, he led me to a tiny room filled with print files and briefly taught me how to catalog paintings. I had envisioned myself with a wooden gavel, bellowing, "I hear two million, who will bid three!" and drinking champagne at Francis Bacon retrospectives. It didn't occur to me that a nonpaying job, that required effusive pleading on my mother's part, would result in a summer boxed in a back room with a magnifying glass and a Sharpie, scrutinizing watercolors.

I would walk home from my airless nook every afternoon making up stories about how I was part of the royal family, but pretending to be a commoner to see what mainstream life was like. Or I was Hungarian and had escaped just after the war, leaving behind the man I loved—but who, I knew, I would one day bump into on the streets of London. Once or twice I was a sexy British spy prepared at any moment to rip off my Sears raincoat and reveal a leather bra and a loaded gun. Am I the only one that does this?

I had dinner with our family friends every night, complete with silver flatware and floral china that corresponded with each course. I would whisper under my breath, "Water glass to the right, bread plate to the left." It was so English and so civilized I sometimes found myself using words like "jolly good," "blimey," and "keep your pecker up" (be happy).

———— ✺ ————

The second day of work, Mr. Talbot scolded me for wearing trousers. I was wearing Ralph Lauren herringbone tweed pants with a white silk blouse; we weren't talking Daisy Duke jean cutoffs and a neon tube top. But pants were forbidden for women by the Christie's dress code. I spent the day in my capsule of boredom feeling like a rebellious Marlene Dietrich before heading out for another jaunt through the park. As I marched past Buckingham Palace, I decided the next day I would wear pasties and crotchless panties; after all, that was what Gloria Steinem would do, right? By dinner (sole meunière and buttered new potatoes) I had calmed down. I decided to forgo a political stand in favor of keeping my professional life intact. But he was a cheeky bastard.

The third day, I was reprimanded again, this time for wearing my hair down. Again, I didn't bunny-hop into one of London's most prestigious establishments looking like Lady Gaga; my hair was simply brushed out and pushed back behind my ears. Christie's women, I was informed, had to wear their hair up in a bun or some kind of Danish. I was never given a reason; I mean, why not a hairnet? I used paper clips to keep my hair in the best croissant I could muster without a brush or mirror, which set the metal detector off coming back from lunch. Let them think I was stealing office supplies. Bugger off.

After work one afternoon, I decided to explore Harrods, the luxury department store I'd been hearing about at work—an enormous five-acre structure that housed everything from truffles and teeth whitener to an elliptical treadmill, a leather mahjong board, and thousands of diamond trinkets. There was even a real miniature black Mercedes for children. Well, Arab children. I loved watching the Saudi princesses come into the store in a cluster of burkas, *hijabs*, and *khumar*. Clearly, while bowing backward out the door, they had told their husbands they were going to the open market to buy turnips. What they did instead was take the white Bentley straight to Harrods, their daytime playground. They would all bundle into the elevator, and "ding"—Ladies' Lingerie. And there the gang stripped down to their Versace bras and panties, drank champagne and smoked Benson & Hedges Lights, and gossiped about Michael Caine and Joan Collins. After hours of doubling for extras out of a Robert Palmer video, they would spray themselves with Lysol and chew a few breath mints, get back into their black habits, and scuttle home. This was the original housewives' reality show.

On my fourth day of work, Mr. Talbot, who clearly needed a kitten in his life, screamed at me yet again—this time for my choice of earrings. I was wearing hoops, and only diamond and pearl studs were acceptable. Why? I thought. As far as I could tell, there weren't many girl gang wars under way at Christie's. I had spent an hour comparing two watercolors of haystacks when from down the hall I heard a holler. "Alexandra!" I froze. First of all, Christie's was a silent institution; second, how many Alexandras could there be? And third, who the hell was screaming out my name?

I gingerly walked into Mr. Talbot's office like a geisha at her debut. "Did you call me?" I said, practically bowing.

"Yes. I would like a lapsang souchong tea with lemon."

I didn't know how to interpret this. "That sounds good, sir." I think I even bowed again.

"No, I want you to get me a tea with lemon."

I spent the next two hours trying to find tea and master the pronunciation of *lapsang souchong*. At last I placed the tea on Mr. Talbot's desk. "He's gone to lunch," I heard from the adjoining room. A ginger-haired woman was holding up slides of Cézanne fruit bowls to the window.

"I'm sorry?" I said, adding a hint of British accent like Madonna.

"Mr. Talbot has gone for his lunch. It's twelve noon." She acted like it was common knowledge that Mr. Talbot took his lunch at twelve noon. Why, that's the reason Big Ben tolls. I was steamed the whole walk home. Sod it. I started planning my own Boston tea party.

On the fifth day, I spent the morning on sixteenth-century pastoral scenes. Green trees, two sheep; green trees, four sheep, and a cow; six sheep, two cows, and five geese. And so on. Suddenly I heard it again: "Al-exandra!" I threw down my artist eraser. I marched down the hallway with purpose, but no ideas. When I entered Mr. Talbot's office, he didn't look up. "Tea."

"Please?" I answered jokingly.

He looked up at me like I had just thrown a dart at Mona Lisa's face. "You're excused."

I could feel my cheeks burning. I tapped my pencil on a Gainsborough drawing so forcefully that I almost tore right through a picnic scene. I gathered the papers and piled them neatly, placed the pencils meticulously in the desk drawer, and slipped out the back stairs.

As I skipped through the park, I felt that one of my many fantasies could in fact be coming true. I was in a different country; I could be anyone. Kitty Kat would be my new name. The next day I took off to Italy with ten gay men, which proved a lot more educational than any internship. I went from viewing John Singer Sargent watercolors to statues of nude Roman men. And going from being alone in a windowless room at an auction house to watching my impeccably groomed traveling companions frolic in the waters of Lido Beach in Venice is eye-opening in its own way.

CHAPTER ELEVEN

what color is my parachute?

Why does everyone drink through college? I would think the time to intoxicate is when you're in your forties, have a mundane job, are beyond baby-bearing, and life just isn't going to change, give or take a few peaks and valleys. But when I was in college, in the apex of youth and promise, everybody was wasted from 6:00 p.m. on. There were these incredible guest writers, artists, and inventors who would sacrifice their SoHo lofts or Marin County houseboats to guest teach, but the student body was either too drunk or too hungover to care, much less show up for a lecture on quantum poetry. Look, I can understand a few beers after the opening of the play or after ten hours in the library, but total intoxication from sunset to sunrise? I really took offense when my college boyfriend got so drunk he peed all over my stereo. Why not the pile of clothes a foot away? Or, dare I say, the damn toilet?

My senior year at Bard, I rented a church with two other people I had never met; with not enough Methodist followers in the area, it had been leased out to college students. My room was in the sanctuary; my bed stood where the altar had been, which made for fascinating dreams and a chaste semester. When my alarm went off in the morning, I would open my eyes to a pensive John the Apostle looking down at me through a prism of colored glass.

I spent my time at the theater with men who wore duct-tape ballet shoes and armless sweatshirts and pirouetted across the cement quad to class. And drama girls who were overly earnest with pale skin and ponchos, always trying to ignite theater games like Accepting Circle and Fast Food Stanislavski. And then there were my friends; one was writing her thesis on the question, "If Hitler had been successful as an artist, would there have been no war?" Or another who spent all day pouring paint on enormous canvases to signify the frailty of the human condition. They lived on Red Stripe beer and stir-fry tofu. It was very hip to be poor and scrappy. Even if you had an allowance from your parents or worked part-time in the admissions office, you still bought wholesale blocks of cheese (lunch for a month) and clothes from the local Goodwill and drove the rustiest, smokiest Dukes of Hazzard dump that could (hopefully) make it through one semester.

And that was how I spent my twentieth year, wearing blousy dresses discarded from relatives of dead women and choking down tempeh. If I had some extra change for maybe a new towel or a steak, I kept it on the down-low. I never out-and-out lied about my background, but my classmates somehow got the impression that I was raised with my siblings in a VW bus traveling around Peru.

It wasn't performing a completely different person so much as tailoring the truth. I found in college, as I would in Hollywood, that my upbringing was irrelevant to who I was, and that less was more when divulging facts about what made me, me. I couldn't be an artist because my parents paid full tuition? I have enough change for laundry, so I'm not grunge? Even though nobody fought it when I treated everyone to gourmet hazelnut coffee beans and real maple syrup.

———— ∽ ————

The only other time in my life I chose not to accurately represent my background is when I was trying to land a job on the sketch comedy show *In Living Color* a few years after I graduated. I was told by my agent, who worked out of his one-room apartment and had a metal index-card box of contacts (two cards), that *In Living Color* was looking for a "black guy to replace Damon Wayans." So, naturally, who better than me? I begged for an audition. And was turned down repeatedly. "But

I'm a character actress! Have you seen my Ben Vereen?" I responded. Finally, I was given an opportunity to humiliate myself. It helped that I was my agent's only client; apparently he harassed the receptionist at the casting agency until she broke down in tears.

I arrived in a black dress the size of a cocktail napkin, with a duffel full of dime-store wigs, costumes, and a ghetto blaster with a cassette of the James Bond theme music. I performed six original monologues, the final of which concluded with me hurling myself against the wall and falling into a heap on the floor. Well, having no shame paid off, and after weeks of performing for every Fox TV Armani suit–wearing executive, my final step was to meet Oz himself, Keenen Ivory Wayans (creator and star). Now this was a comedy show that ridiculed white people, and white women were the comedic bottom feeders. I wasn't going to meet Keenen as some Debbie Debutante with a monogrammed blazer and topsiders. No, not when the show had musical guests who sang lyrics like "kill whitey." I wore a polyester miniskirt, stiletto heels, and a tube top with a unicorn on it. (Keenen later told people I wasn't wearing any underwear, but that is not true; what if I were in a car accident on the way home?) I smacked gum, swore like a truck-stop whore, and wore stiletto boots that made me walk like a newborn colt.

When I found out I'd gotten the job, my agent and I were so ecstatic, we both ran tiny victory laps around his studio.

My mother didn't understand the show's brand of humor, but then again, she wasn't the target audience. She used to ask me why I wasn't working on a movie with Meryl Streep, like it was my choice. I must note here that recently I had the privilege and luck of playing in a film alongside Meryl Streep. (And from that moment on, my mother referred to me as her "actress," and not "her other daughter.") Perhaps because I played many strippers and prostitutes (nothing my college performances of Chekhov and Brecht had prepared me for), when I wasn't working I preserved whatever humility I had left. I had plenty of rest. I had a balanced breakfast. So when Tupac shot his driver at one of our tapings or a guest star flashed me in his dressing room, I could power through such moments with composure that would have made my mother proud. And when not dressed in a stripper thong and pasties, I was my usual modest self. Or at least I tried. One day I had to go to my annual gynecological appointment. I called the stage manager and told him I would be late for rehearsal because I was taking my dog to the vet. When I returned from my appointment, I walked onstage to find the cast and crew getting ready to rehearse a Jim Carrey sketch. The stage manager spotted me and yelled, "Hey! How's your pooch?"

Eventually my repertoire of scantily dressed characters expanded into celebrity impersonations. I was given the opportunity to play such famous women as

Cindy Crawford, Sharon Stone, Hillary Clinton, and Cher. I found it challenging and exciting to morph into real people and capture their idiosyncrasies and characteristics. One day, a production assistant from the office came skipping onto the set with a letter from Cher. Well, of course I assumed she wanted to meet for sushi in Malibu or maybe cut an album together. At the very least, invite me to come backstage at her next Vegas show!

I ripped open the envelope: "Kiss my ass, Cher."

Never fly too close to the flame.

It was embarrassing, when discussing my background with directors, to confess that I hadn't taken a Greyhound bus from Cisco, Texas, where I was the prettiest girl in Podunk and knew in my heart I was a star. I met a lot of those "gals" along the way, and don't have the most optimistic feeling about where some of them are today. What is the shelf life of an escort? The subtext of my childhood, however, seemed to be "You're from a middle-class family, you are privileged"; people assumed that I had just enough money in the bank to stamp out the will to work and extinguish any fire in my well-fed belly. But I didn't know a soul in Hollywood, and nobody wanted to sleep with me, so I couldn't screw my way to the middle. I had to do it with perseverance and a sprinkle of talent. And one of the great things about *In Living Color* was, it allowed me to "play against type." After the show was canceled, I was only considered for Suzy Chapstick and debutante parts.

Even as recently as this year, I met with the producers of *Law & Order SVU*, who were thinking of me for a Harvard grad prosecutor. I pleaded with them, "Please, just once, can I play a murderous, psychopathic crack whore?"

They couldn't see it.

"Fine, then what about a black guy?"

CHAPTER TWELVE

the four seasons

Most mothers love to dispense sage, timeworn advice to their children. You attract more flies with honey, a penny saved is a penny earned, when you are stressed close your eyes and think of Christmas . . . My mother shared all these chestnuts with me. But the one piece of advice that is embedded in my mind and has, consequently, determined the outcome of many key moments of my life is hers and hers alone: "Just go to the Four Seasons."

The Four Seasons has always been a safe haven for our family. It's one of those silk-curtained, velvet couch places that instantly puts my mother at ease. She could have tea there, get her hair blown out and overly sprayed, and maybe take a night off from the puking kids. One of the biggest fights I ever had with my older sister culminated with us meeting at the Four Seasons for Earl Grey tea, raisin scones, and a three-hour relationship analysis. My mother thought it the appropriate meeting place, like a Park Ave. psychiatrist's office without the Freudian shrink and the African masks, but with a great Caesar salad. We had many lunches there, dinners, breakfasts celebrating birthdays, snow days, good days, and bad days.

I was living in Los Angeles with my boyfriend Felix, an Italian man-child with huge almond eyes and callused hands. He was a carpenter and a potter. Felix was one of sixteen children (no twins) from Poughkeepsie, New York. His mother was an Italian Catholic, understatement of the year, and he was lucky number thirteen. There was always a basket of shoes by the front door and whoever got out the door the quickest would be guaranteed a matching pair of shoes. If you were one of the last, you'd be ridiculed by classmates for wearing one size 8 men's slipper and one toddler size flip-flop. Sunday supper consisted of twenty people in the immediate family and around thirty-two babies. That's a lot of boiled potatoes.

I met him my senior year in college. He had just graduated and was home waiting tables at a local Mexican restaurant. A place I frequented and, after taking one look at him, a place I begged for a job at. I was not only loaded down with schoolwork, a senior thesis, and roles in the school plays, but my parents gave me a stipend to pay for incidentals. The last thing I needed was to hoist twenty margaritas on a tray over my head and serve drunken college students until three in the morning. Oh, but his eyes …

My shift never coincided with his and the job was becoming all-consuming. Finally, I switched shifts with another waitress so I could have my moment with him. Unfortunately, he switched with someone as well and I was stuck with a waiter with a severe halitosis problem. Felix had the audacity to saunter into the restaurant at the end of the evening with pals for a beer and I confronted him like a jilted lover and not the absolute stranger that, in reality, I was.

"You owe me a beer, fucker!" was my sophisticated opening line. Aggressive? Yes, but remember what I said about being a python.

Felix moved to L.A. a few months after I did because we missed each other and, let's face it, you can build shelves anywhere. He drove an olive green Volare with a smashed-in passenger side door. Your basic garden-variety death trap.

My mother lost sleep at the idea of me cruising around in that car, which was basically a microwave on wheels. She decided to sell her new Subaru to Felix for $1,000. I had to convince him she wasn't doing this because she pitied him; she just hated the color—midnight blue. He never knew she bought the same car in midnight blue months later. But for her it was money well spent.

Felix and I lived in a bungalow with a little garden in the Hollywood section of Los Angeles. If I were scouting a location for a film about a couple who was struggling in the arts, but spiritually lifted by growing their own zucchini and hiking at sunset, this would be the place. I would also cast Gisele Bündchen to play me. We rescued a dog named Trout and had small dinners for other wannabe actors, chefs, and writers; the Cowboy Junkies provided our life sound track. Unfortunately it was my damn ambition that tore us apart. I didn't necessarily have to be a film studio head's wife with a face that had been worked on more often than her vintage Jag, but I could no longer handle handing out steel-cut oats at the co-op. I wanted a career. And I hate zucchini.

Felix spent his time throwing pots and glazing earthenware. I had joined a theater company in town called the Groundlings, a sketch comedy troop with a theater in the Melrose district. Every Sunday we would do a show for the public, which involved a variety of wigs and a repertoire of crazy old lady and bimbo model characters. After a show we would all go out and have a beer and regale ourselves with commentary on the brilliance that had been expressed earlier that night. We would desperately try to outfunny each other in the most boisterous and provocative way. And then leave a stingy tip. Lisa Kudrow and Will Ferrell were part of the group; they have since skyrocketed to fame. And I'm happy for them. Really, I am. No, seriously, I am.

One night, a fellow Groundling named Sam walked me to my car, which was parked in the alley behind the theater. It was an ominous little patch of concrete where you were bound to trip on a syringe or a sleeping homeless woman who would call you Uncle Pie and swing her fist at the air. We needed to schedule rehearsal times and decide who was going to buy the fake blood and whipped cream. I remember a shadow flying by the corner of my eye, like one of the birds in a

Hitchcock film. The next second, eight *cholos*, Mexican gang members with hairnets and tattoos, had us surrounded, knives and screwdrivers pressed against our necks. I instantly put my head down, thinking that if I couldn't identify them in court, maybe they wouldn't hurt us. I was shoved and poked as they rifled through my car (the blue Subaru), tossing a rainbow clown wig and half a Big Mac onto the pavement. I repeated over and over, "I don't have any money. I never take my wallet to the theater because, you know, actors!" I couldn't tell if they didn't speak English or were too high on crack to engage in conversation.

At one point I was taken to the trunk of the car, my arms firmly planted on the back windshield, as they began lining up behind me. Then there was a lot of yelling in Spanish, and I was pushed toward the front of the car again. I don't know what happened or why they changed their minds, but I'm grateful to the one member who wasn't in the mood that night and persuaded them to forgo a gang rape. The cops later told me that this particular gang would abduct people, take them to Griffith Park, rape and dismember them, and dispose of their limbs in the park Dumpsters. I never envisioned the end of my life being so local-newsy.

The passenger door was opened (if it had been the Volare, this all would have been over much sooner), and just as I was beginning to lower myself into the seat, I looked over at Sam. He mouthed the words, "Don't get in." It was as if he'd snapped his fingers and woken me from my passive trance. I suddenly realized that if I entered the car, I would never exit. Thank God for survival instincts; you never know you have them until those rare moments when they're challenged.

I turned and ran my ass off. Two of the gang members chased me. I've never been a jock (spin class literally makes me faint), but my adrenaline kicked in with such force, I would have given Jesse Owens a run for his money. I made it to Melrose Avenue and stood in the middle of the road trying to stop cars and screaming for help. Cars swerved around me, moving past like I was some *Twin Peaks* character they were hallucinating. As I looked down the alley, I saw the gang stabbing my friend Sam in the chest.

Finally a man walking his Australian sheepdog and sipping a cappuccino came to my rescue. He started yelling in a heavy Croatian accent and running toward Sam. At that point the gang jumped into my Subaru and screeched away. My hero called the police.

Sam, as it turns out, was wearing his jean jacket with the thick fleece underneath—you know, the kind country singers wear? The blades had gotten stuck in the fleece, which made the wounds less severe than they might have been. I will never, ever call fleece-lined denim jackets redneck again.

The ambulance whisked us to the Cedars-Sinai Medical Center. Sam had minor surgery and a multitude of stitches. I collapsed in the waiting room and cried harder than I ever had. It wasn't the sad cry of PMS; it was more of a primal scream, like when passing a kidney stone. "Do you want to use the phone?" the nurse asked me. When you're in semi-shock, it's difficult to decide who to call. I thought about Lee Majors, because he could lift my car up and shake those bad guys out like pepper flakes onto the cement freeway. I thought about Felix, but I knew a hug and a mug of homemade licorice spice tea wouldn't comfort me. I called my mother. The feeling of wanting one's mommy is a feeling I don't think any human outgrows. There are times when I'd crawl right back in that womb, if she'd let me.

It was surreal to hear myself tell the story as if I were recounting a movie I had just seen. I screamed the words "rape," "gang," and "stabbed" over and over. There was a pause. "Go to the Four Seasons!" she said firmly. And you know what—I didn't question it. Of course! I thought.

The next morning I took Sam, bandaged and high on Percocet, directly from the ER exit to Suite 402 in the Beverly Hills Four Seasons. We stayed for two weeks. There was room service, laps in the Olympic-size pool, and a daily phone call with a post-traumatic stress therapist. Her professional advice, thousands of dollars' worth of talk later, was for me to buy a stuffed animal—a friend who would give me unconditional love. She became one of a string of therapists that I should have reported to the psychoanalytic board. With the money I spent talking to these imbeciles, I could have bought an island in the Maldives, and then I would never have had cause to be depressed again.

—— ✦ ——

From that point on the Four Seasons became my mecca for a quiet mind, my ashram of calm. If Eloise had narrowly escaped a gang rape or was coming off heroin, I'm sure she would take to the Plaza the same way. Sam never questioned why he was sleeping at the Four Seasons. I guess trauma had rendered him mute. If I was eating at a luxury hotel on somebody else's tab, I probably wouldn't question it either.

Shortly after the trauma, Felix and I broke up, and, as happens when people experience such a thing together, Sam and I briefly dated. Trauma brings couples together, but we were short-lived. It turns out a harrowing ordeal isn't enough to keep two people together. Oh . . . and he was gay.

It's curious to me that my parents never actually flew out to L.A. to see me after this. Perhaps without an actual rape or severed jugular, it wasn't worth spending the miles. I did get a bouquet of lilies from a friend of my mother's. I think she misunderstood and thought I'd died.

—— ✦ ——

Years later another tragedy struck, this one a little less personal: 9/11. I was newly engaged and in New York to apartment-hunt. I was moving from L.A. to New York, and my fiancé had to give up his bachelor pad (and all that implied). I was excited to leave the California wheatgrass shots and avocado face masks behind me and dive into the dirt and grit of urban living.

The planes had struck the Twin Towers while I was still sleeping. I woke up and turned the kettle and TV on. In my stupor I assumed the Twin Towers burning on the screen were a scene from some crappy Bruckheimer film, and as I flipped the channels, I couldn't understand why at a peak news hour all networks were choosing to show the same movie. But after five minutes without a glimpse of Nicolas Cage's glistening muscles, I knew it was real.

I went out to West Eighty-second Street to witness faint smoke wafting from downtown and people rushing in different directions the way ants do when you pour water on them. Cell phones and landlines weren't working. I was desperate to reach my fiancé, George, and find out where he was. (He was climbing out of a smoke-filled subway. But that's his book.) I suddenly felt the vibration of my cell phone in my pocket. The one person who had managed to crash through the technology pileup? My mother. "Are you okay?"

We spoke quickly, knowing that the connection could be lost at any moment. "Where's George?"

"Not sure, I assume at work."

"You need to get him, and the two of you go right to the Four Seasons!"

Let me explain the geography of this proposal. If the island of Manhattan were a naked lady, we were already safely ensconced in her collarbone; 9/11 hit her calf, and my mother suggested we go down and stay in the belly button. Nonsensical? Yes. Did we do it? Yes! I was so emphatic that George didn't question me. But if you're going to witness the apocalypse, isn't it better with room service?

Recently there was a blizzard in Manhattan that dropped twenty inches in Central Park. From our living room window we watched nature's spectacular show of snow, wind, and lightning. My kids were thrilled at the prospect of being snowed in. Me, I began to sweat at the prospect of cheese fondue and Candyland for ten days. All the old ladies had thought ahead and bought up all the yogurt and bran flakes from our local D'Agostino. I panicked. "Shouldn't we go to the Four Seasons?" George pointed out that our apartment was bigger than a hotel room, nicer, and housed all our books and toys. The last thing I needed at that moment was practical reasoning. He and the girls headed out for some prime sledding while I, in pajamas, dirty hair held together with a pencil, frantically called the Four Seasons several blocks away. Needless to say, actual out-of-towners were stranded, and the hotel was full to capacity.

We made it through that week with minimal cannibalism and no divorce proceedings. I have the creators of Wii to thank. And like a meth addict going through detox, I had sweated out the idea that the five-star hotel was my only life raft.

But don't get me wrong; on my deathbed, when my family and friends come to pay their last respects, I'll be in the presidential suite. At the Four Seasons. In Nevis.

CHAPTER THIRTEEN

ali in
wonderland

I had always been skittish living with my friend Anne up in the Hollywood Hills. Two salient details led to repeated bouts with insomnia: one, the house was near where the Manson murders had taken place; and two, we were renting the house from Robert Englund (aka Freddy Krueger in the *Night mare on Elm Street* series). One afternoon I was looking to store some broken speakers in the garage when I came upon a rubber Freddy Krueger mask and was so horrified I tried to break our lease. What was even more frightening was that the mask was more attractive than most of the men I was dating at the time.

The house was built into a hill that was straight up Laurel Canyon and off Wonderland Avenue. During the rainy months we carried our tea and yogurt from the kitchen to the living room through a heavy stream of mud. There was one bedroom upstairs, which was the clear winner, with a skylight and a view of the street, and a downstairs bedroom that smelled like mildew, was riddled with spiders, and had a sliding glass door that opened onto a pile of dirt. The upstairs bedroom could be a tree house in Costa Rica; the bottom bedroom looked like the dank basements where police find skulls of missing prostitutes. Anne and I did what all sophisticated and mature women would do to determine the bedroom assignment: Rock, Paper, Scissors. I lost. We decided to swap every six months, and I started in the dungeon first. I willed myself to be rational. What were the odds a mentally ill man would climb Laurel Canyon, target our house, and slit my throat? Better than I thought.

I decided to place the bed against the sliding glass door—a sort of modernist headboard. At night when I stared up from my bed, I could almost make out a patch of sky. Six months after moving in, I was lying in my bed next to my dog, Trout. Trout was the love of my life. He was a yellow lab mutt who went everywhere with me, forced me to exercise (HE took ME on hikes), and slept in my bed so I could spoon him like a pregnancy pillow. I often wondered, If Trout had been a man, would we have been soul mates? Would he look like Matt Damon? And then I would be disturbed by how icky that thought was. He was my pet! Plus, he had no money.

So Trout was in a deep, muscle-spasm-filled sleep, and I was trying to find the little patch of sky while

mulling over how to tell a married Hollywood pro-
ducer to stop leaving me filthy messages. Suddenly
a scraggly, bearded face appeared directly above my
head. He was peering in the glass door; he hadn't noticed me yet. I sprang up and began screaming; Trout
jumped up and began snarling. The demonic figure
began fiddling with the door handle.

I ran out of the bedroom, taking every third stair
as I raced to alert my roommate. "Anne! Anne! Call
nine-one-one," I belted as I tore through to the
kitchen. I was wearing little boy shorts and a tank top,
perfect slasher-film attire. I grabbed the only knife
we had, a dull yard-sale bread knife. I would not be
the slut who gets gored by a machete. Anne leisurely
opened her bedroom door as if I had sung, "Coffee's
ready!"

Meanwhile, Trout was snarling and barking like
he was in the middle of an illegal dogfight. "There's a
man downstairs! A man just broke in, and he's going
to kill us!"

Anne was still half asleep. "What do you mean, a
man? Do you know him?"

This was not the time for Anne's Harvard education to ignite some line of logical reasoning. "Call the
police, or we're gonna die," I shouted as we heard my
side table crash and Trout growling like he had a limb
in his mouth. Anne ran to her room to call 911.

A minute later, all was quiet. Trout padded up
and assumed his usual position by the back door. He

was not going to chase the intruder into the hills; he needed to pee.

When the police finally showed up, they blinded me with their flashlights, as if the first thing on the agenda was to see if I was some paranoid actress strung out on diet pills. I showed them my room, which could have passed for a crime scene on *CSI*. The sliding glass door was wide open, and my underwear was strewn all over the floor.

"Any chance the dog did this?" one of the cops asked.

"He's brilliant, but I've never seen him stand up and pull the sliding door open, he's indifferent to my panties, AND I SAW THE MAN!"

"Could you have been dreaming?" the other cop queried while pretending to scribble on some official pad.

"I was awake, I saw a man with a beard who looked like Jesus Christ. But mean."

The scribbling cop looked up. "Any chance it was?" Both cops guffawed in unison. Anne had never heard or seen a thing, so she stood watching the exchange with a concerned and silent look, like she was at Centre Court at Wimbledon.

The next morning a cop with no gun or credentials (an intern or the Xeroxer, no doubt) came to dust for prints on the glass door. The actors in *Police Academy* do a better job impersonating the law than this guy. He said things like, "We'll run the prints and see if we get a match." But they never did. I probably never even rated a file.

—————— ◌◌ ——————

My mother arrived a few days later. She had been in San Francisco for work and stopped in Los Angeles to visit. Over toast and fresh orange juice at the Four Seasons, I regaled my mother and brother with my near-death story. "Don't you think it was just a neighbor who got lost?" my mother asked.

I had to embellish a little to convey the horror of the situation. "He was this deranged man with blood all over his beard, holding a knife."

"Isn't there an alarm?" my mother asked.

"Mom, the house could have been built by Habitat for Humanity—it barely has running water."

"Well," she answered, "this is an issue for your landlord. I believe contractually he has to put in an alarm." She seemed to make sense; however, Robert Englund was in Transylvania filming a straight-to-DVD movie, and we had no forwarding number. "I think you should put in an alarm and bill him when he gets back."

"Mom, I can't do that. We would have to get his permission, and he's away for the next six months. I mean, otherwise people would add guesthouses and water slides and just bill their landlord."

My mother was adamant that I should be more equipped in case the serial killer or maybe a friend of the serial killer decided to pay another visit. I was secretly hoping she would yank me out of the house and spring for a condo on the tenth floor in Beverly Hills. Instead, my mother and I went to a local hardware store in West Los Angeles. She got a cart and started wheeling it around the home improvement section. She threw in locks, a flashlight, rope (to calf-rope him, rodeo style?), and a million other things until the cart was full. There was even a toilet plunger; I wasn't sure if this was meant to double as a weapon. One of my favorite accoutrements was a knife she bought to hide under my bed. It was a knife used for gutting fish, sharp, with serrated teeth. My expertise in human disembowelment was minimal; I had no idea how I would use it unless I was in Guadeloupe and had a red snapper splashing on the line. She placed it under my bed along with a whistle and the rope. (What would I do first—blow the whistle, decimate his insides, or tie his ankles and wrists together?) I don't think Anne, who was just upstairs, could even hear the whistle when we had our practice run.

The last thing my mother set up on the table next to my bed was a panic button. "This is very important. When you see or hear something, you press this button, and it immediately alerts the police." I breathed a sigh of relief. Finally, something that was practical and a functioning lifesaver.

• • •

I slept that night with my mother at the Four Seasons; I mean, why not, when given the choice? Plus, we were running low on shampoo and toilet paper. The next day she flew back to Washington, and I returned to Amityville Horror. The more the story got around, the more I was questioned. "Are you sure you saw someone? Maybe your mind was playing tricks?" My mind doesn't play tricks. I saw a man that night, it was a fin in the ocean that time in Bermuda, and that guy Steve had eyes on his penis.

A few nights later, Trout and I were cuddling in my bed, my hand inches away from the knife as I mentally mapped out an escape route should a rapist come a-knocking. Anne was at her boyfriend's house, so I was alone, the ideal target for any deranged caller. I finally nodded off, but was awakened just before dawn. Somebody was trying to break in on the side of the house. Trout kept snoring no matter how hard I nudged him (he had eaten a pack of raw bacon). The noise continued; my killer had come back, this time with Squeaky Fromme.

It escaped me, that morning, that it was the weekly ritual of trash pickup. I was normally asleep at this hour, and not on the alert for a cult murder scheme.

I groped around for the panic button and pushed it. I pushed it again and again. And then waited for the sirens.

The sun came up, cars started to drive up the hill,

and Trout did his morning stretch. I was still trembling, my stomach in knots. Where were the police? The hovering chopper? The German shepherds patrolling the yard? Dear Lord, I was almost hacked to death!

I picked up the panic button. It was light and plastic. I shook it and pushed the button several times. I then read the back. The button was part of an elaborate home alarm system. Once a professional had installed the wiring, the main alarm, and created a password, the button (which required four AAA batteries) was then synchronized with the system. The button would trigger the alarm, which would alert the police via the system's computer program.

Maybe my mother didn't know that? Perhaps she, like me, assumed the button would do what it was supposed to do and alert the authorities? Or maybe she was giving me a little piece of pretend plastic to ward away any other ghosts and goblins that might want to violate my overproductive imagination? Either way, as this was twenty years ago, somewhere in the hills of Los Angeles there's an elderly serial killer with a walker hobbling loose.

CHAPTER FOURTEEN

french kiss-off

I believe that every woman should sample all the different groups in the male food pyramid. That way, when you finally get married, you're never enticed by the fantasy of the sculpted yoga instructor who "gets you" or the Brazilian ex-husband of a gallery owner you met once at a Ben Nicholson retrospective. You've been there, you've done him. Marriage is like being on a perpetual fast, in that you don't have to waste all that time fantasizing about the curly fries if you've had them already. And barfed.

Thierry was a French director—to be specific, my director on an independent movie he was shooting in L.A. He wasn't the unlaundered, bewhiskered Coen brothers indie type; he was dapper, wore Prada sunglasses, and swaggered around like he was the next Kubrick. He was a former fashion photographer who had grown bored of fornication with vapid models and long weeks in the Caribbean shooting perky breasts dusted with white sand. He was the privileged son of a Paris financier and possessed all the attributes of a spoiled European. At nineteen, he had a drug problem. When I asked him how it happened, he simply replied: "[*Strong French accent*] What do you mean, how? I was an artist!" Call me naive, but wouldn't a sketch class or an investment in a kiln have done the trick? When Thierry's parents discovered he was an addict, they sent him to Saint Lucia for a year to dry out. If I were smacked out, my mother would sit in a room with me reading *The Prime of Miss Jean Brodie* and spooning me cream of tomato soup. And it would take half the time.

It was in the second month of filming that I realized Thierry was smitten. I played a lawyer in the movie, yet he kept requesting that wardrobe dress me in lingerie. He pushed for nudity in ludicrous scenes, including my final argument to the jury. I finally relented and did a scene in a bubble bath wearing a skin-colored one-piece bathing suit. (Surprisingly, that scene was cut out of the movie.) On the last night of shooting he came knocking on my trailer door. An American man would have said something like, "Hey, can I take you out for a burger?" But the Frenchman opened with "[*Strong French accent*] I want to make love to you." I explained I didn't make sex with anyone who hadn't logged in at least a hundred hours of chat time. But I have to admit, his persistence was seductive. We had a couple of intimate dinners (with no making sex).

The film wrapped, and Thierry flew back to Paris

to edit. I was pretty certain that was that. I wouldn't see him at any awards shows or press junkets; even Leonard the crafts service guy knew the movie was going straight to video. After the second week of shooting Leonard stopped passing out homemade enchiladas and just left a bowl of pretzels next to the restroom.

A couple weeks later, however, Thierry called and begged me to fly to Paris. It would be my first trip there as an adult. My mother was always telling me about the exquisiteness of Paris. She spent her junior year at Smith in France, and it was her Sputnik moment. I needed fashionable clothes, was obsessed with steak frites, and had never been to the Musée Rodin. And he was sexy. I also relished the idea of being unpredictable and un-bridled. So I said yes. I figured I could keep the making sex at bay at least until I hit the Porte de Clignancourt flea market and collected more of those porcupine quill boxes. There's no such thing as a free coach ticket.

The best part of the trip was the anticipation on the flight over. I wore sweatpants, but my carry-on held a revealing black Dolce & Gabbana blouse and fitted jeans. I was going to strut off the plane like Brigitte Bardot entering a party in Capri, just without the hair, the ass, or the boobs.

Thierry picked me up in a slate-colored, dented Citroen, something you could find on French eBay. His apartment was tiny, but mod (read: small), and featured black-and-white nudes of the Icelandic model he lived with before she told him she was pregnant with his baby and he kicked her out. I found the four-foot-high studio photographs of Lina's perfectly manicured vagina slightly off-putting, but chalked it up to cultural differences. Maybe my vagina deserved at least a wallet size? The apartment was minimalist—bohemian chic with whitewashed parquet floors, and a rickety staircase that led to a loft bed. One tiny bathroom with a toilet the size of a four-quart stockpot and a shower stall so tight you couldn't bathe a hamster in it.

The few days I was in Paris, I played the kind of role I was never cast as—the sensuous ingenue. We watched a Woody Allen marathon in the rain one Sunday afternoon in the sixteenth arrondissement, ate Ethiopian food with our hands, and exchanged lascivious glances as we browsed French bookstores. We improvised Anaïs Nin and Henry Miller even when we made sex. French men are absurdly romantic, for a time, before they lose interest and hop onto the next glistening lily pad. Thierry would whisper lines to me like, "I'm hungry for the food of your love," and "I'm going to take you to the moon," while I gorged on coq au vin and mustered up enigmatic replies like, "Please pass the bread."

By the time he drove me to Charles de Gaulle Airport a week later, we were in real pretend love, Hollywood-style. Back in Los Angeles, I felt too European for my circle of friends. After all, I had been in Paris for a week, and my boyfriend's French lineage dated back to Marie Antoinette. I needed to be with Gérard Depardieu and Catherine Deneuve and the people of my new tribe. I needed to smoke more and eat unpasteurized cheese that smelled like feet. I bought *French for Dummies* and started over-gesticulating.

I began the ritual of flying back and forth from L.A. to Paris as if I was commuting from Scarsdale to Manhattan (and my credit card bills were showing it). I knew the market, shops, and cafés in Thierry's neighborhood and became an independent American in Paris (within a hundred-yard radius). I delighted at the illuminated Arc de Triomphe at night, wept walking through the Père Lachaise Cemetery, and wondered if my mother tried the same steak tartare from Closerie des Lilas, or wore a flowing gown on the back of a motorcycle. She probably experienced many of my adventures, just without the sex.

The first red flag in the torrid love affair was raised at a farm in Normandy, where we'd driven for a romantic weekend. I was struck by the impulse to ride a horse bareback down the beach (I've always been obsessed with "Dover Beach," the poem about the battle of Normandy—"where ignorant armies clash at night"). Thierry rolled his eyes, content to recline in the inn's Pratesi sheets. I was so relentless, however, that he called an old friend, Etienne, who happened to own a horse farm nearby. It turned out Etienne was a retired, straight hairdresser who used to trade Argentinian models with Thierry like base-ball cards.

When we arrived at the estate, I explained to the overly groomed men that I hadn't ridden in years, didn't have proper riding boots, and was envisioning a plump pony like the kind at petting zoos or kids' birthday parties. Suddenly an enormous black horse was led out, so gigantic, I expected hundreds of tiny Greek men with swords to come popping out of its rib cage. This uncastrated equine specimen was being trained for the Olympics.

"He's a beauty," I said, "but there's no way I can handle him." Believe me, this horse would have had Catherine the Great double-crossing her legs.

Thierry lifted his Prada sunglasses onto his high-lighted hair: "[*Strong French accent*] What are you say-ing? I made all this effort! We are here! Get on the horse!"

I tried to block out my mother's voice in my head ("Trust your gut"), as every fiber in my body bel-lowed, "Get the hell out of there!" With the help of three stable boys, I was hoisted onto the back of the mighty stud. The horse had two reins, which meant he was such a force he needed four leather belts just to pull his head back. The horse's head being the size of an Acura. Holy *Merde*! (*Shit* in French.)

I started at a slow pace with a sleepy walk around the ring. "Come on, work him," Etienne kept yelling at me. I gave the horse a gentle kick, but he didn't react. The horse knew I was a feeble female without the resources or strength to even comb his mane. I could sense his contempt. Etienne kept yelling. "Let's go, let's go, he's full of blood!" Again I kicked; again, nothing.

Etienne and Thierry walked up to the fence. "[*Strong French accent*] C'mon, ride the damn horse," Thierry chimed in. I made the universal clucking sound that means "Move your ass" in horse. I kicked him so feverishly he reluctantly picked up the pace to a trot, purposely scraping my outside leg against the wood barricade in the process.

"Yes! He's full of blood!" (I never knew what Etienne meant by that; a tick is also full of blood.) The horse started cantering faster and faster until, un-prompted, he turned to approach a five-foot jump in the center of the ring. "Whoa!" I whispered, pulling back the reins until my biceps shook. He snorted, flip-ping his head back as he continued his mad gallop. I could feel his torso rise as my inner thighs simultane-ously slipped down the back of the saddle. My head hit the ground with such force, the sand felt like solid ice. I couldn't breathe for thirty seconds. My skull throbbed; my back was numb.

After what felt like hours, I cautiously sat up. I nat-urally assumed Thierry and Etienne would be run-ning toward me with horror and shame on their faces. I needed to let them know I was alive. I stood up, dusting the evidence off my jeans, and glanced over to where they had been standing in judgment. They had vanished.

I walked toward the gate to witness the two men charging behind the horse, pleading for it to stop as if in some unrequited love drama. If, God forbid, I had been paralyzed from the neck down, I would still be horizontal in the sand outside a baroque village in Normandy today.

———— ❦ ————

Another autumnal weekend Thierry suggested we go to Madrid. There was a black-tie ball at the Ritz-Carlton, and his friends were all going. The gala was basically prom for thirty-year-olds. There was champagne and dancing, and I was content being his armpiece while he switched off between French and Spanish in heated debates about football. (I kept snorting under my breath, "It's called soccer.") And everyone was overly cologned; I had to restrain myself from pointing out that if they showered, they wouldn't need to douse themselves with Eau Sauvage. Thierry took me out to the balcony. I thought we were going to share a cigarette or throw tapas on the people below, but he pulled out a velvet box and smirked. "[*Strong French accent*] I want you to be my wife," he commanded.

Oh, shit. Now here's the thing about being proposed to in a city you don't know, in a country you're not familiar with, filled with people you've never met. You could get stranded in a *Not Without my Daughter* way. It was easier for me to say yes, enjoy the rest of the evening, and figure out an exit strategy later. What if he stole my passport? I couldn't find an ATM? The rest of the evening culminated with his friends frantically hugging us and raising glasses. I was relieved; because of the time difference, we couldn't ring my family with the news. Later that night I threw up all over the polished marble bathroom. "Bad oysters," I said, not that I had had any.

And then it was Thanksgiving, and I was off to Virginia to spend a cold and dreary week with my family at my mother's farm, complete with a red barn and a pond full of slimy carp. I was looking forward to sleeping most of the day, not having to wear makeup or shaving anything. My fantasy was rudely interrupted one morning when Thierry called to inform me that he was flying to Virginia to formally request my hand in marriage. I had forgotten about the whole engagement thing because I hadn't told a soul and was hoping it would just disappear. I thought it would be rude to RSVP no thank you to my own wedding, so I relented and scribbled down his flight info.

Just before I picked him up at the airport, I confessed to my mother that he had proposed. She raised her right eyebrow. "Well, we'll just see about that." Which in Mom-speak meant, "Fat chance."

• • •

An hour later Thierry and I drove up the ramshackle road to the farm. The foliage was dead, the pond frozen in a murky sheet, and the neighbor's foxhound yelped insistently at our car, as if sensing that a European poseur had entered the premises. My family all sat at the kitchen table in anticipation of this François Truffaut character I was bringing home. My older sister was nine months pregnant and wearing pajama bottoms and her husband's sweater covered in toddler spittle. (My brother-in-law was dangling off the tail of a helicopter in Patagonia, shooting a documentary.) My younger sister had a ratty blanket draped around her shoulders, like a Civil War soldier, as she sipped PMS dried raspberry leaf tea (homemade, of course). My older brother was still asleep, and would be for some days. And my mother was busying herself with chores like beeswaxing an old farmhouse table and clearing out cheap glass vases from Valentine's Days gone by. She looked like a normal housewife going about her business, but I knew what was happening. She was preparing for war, sharpening her metaphoric swords and stockpiling her ammunition. Tidying up is my mother's way of mobilizing for battle.

Thierry walked in wearing a black Gucci suit, cashmere coat, checkered scarf, and sunglasses. It was dark outside. My mother gave him the once-over and whispered to my sister, "Is he blind?" I tried to smooth out the awkward meet and greet and scurried up the stairs to take his caramel leather suitcase to the guest room. (My mother was well aware of the shenanigans that went on when we had overnight guests, but she dutifully subscribed to the school of "If I don't see it, it doesn't exist.") Thierry presented my mother with a bottle of Dom Pérignon with a note, "For a weekend of toasts." Oh, Lord.

The next morning I was preparing a tray to bring up to Thierry. Don't judge me, I'm a pleaser. A linen napkin with a pot of coffee, toast, jam, and a little vase with a weed I had snatched from the side of the barn. "What is this?" my mother inquired. My sisters were wearing the exact same clothes as the day before, in the same seats, sipping the same PMS tea.

"I'm bringing Thierry breakfast."

My mother stood. "He doesn't know how to fix his own breakfast?"

I walked out of the room with the rattling tray like the maid in *Remains of the Day*.

At the crack of dawn the next morning my younger sister swung open the door to the guest room and screamed, "Sissy's in labor! Sissy's in LABOR!" Lights were abruptly flicked on, voices got louder, and a frenzy mounted. Only Thierry stayed in bed. We were two hours from Washington, D.C., and my mother and younger sister grabbed some blankets and towels and escorted Sissy into the Audi station wagon. My brother bounded out of the house and leaped into the rolling car. My job was to look after my nephews, ages seven and five, who had just witnessed a bucket of water gush out of their mother's sweatpants.

When Thierry finally descended downstairs, my nephews were spitting chewed marshmallows onto the windowpanes to see if they'd stick. I knew that if the four of us were sequestered in the house all day, somebody would die (the French one). I decided we should all go out and buy baby things for the impending arrival. The crib Sissy had was duct-taped together from the first two kids, so I figured a new crib, blanket, and lots of jingly things would be necessary.

Unfortunately, out in rural Virginia there were no adorable infant boutiques like Posh Tots, Giggles, or Poopies. The only place I knew of was a Kmart forty-five minutes away. We took my brother-in-law's Ford Bronco, which smelled like stale unfiltered Camel cigarettes and had a dried hawk's foot dangling from the rearview mirror. Thierry wiped the seat with a paper towel before sitting, as if he'd contract syphilis through the polyester fibers.

It was impossible to converse with the boys over their fart noises and mock Uzi noises aimed at the passing Deer Crossing signs. Thierry and I stared straight ahead in silence. When we got to Kmart, the boys took off like they were chasing the carrot at a greyhound race. I pleaded with Thierry to follow them so they wouldn't get lost or abducted by creepy farmhands. Kmarts are always massive, but the one we beamed into that morning was the mothership. I was exhausted after perusing just one aisle. The baby section was infinite. There were heaps of boxes with car seats, strollers, bouncing chairs thrown everywhere. Finally a very pregnant Hell's Angel babe with a tattoo of an iguana gracing her protruding belly mounted a pile of stock boxes. She swiped a crib box off the top rack, caught it with the shelf of her stomach, and handed it to me. Who says chivalry is dead.

Two hours later, Thierry appeared, looking pale, as if he had just been probed *Deliverance*-style in the plus-size men's department. "I can't do it," he kept saying over and over. In the corner of my eye I saw my nephews zoom by. They had ripped open a softball set and were using the store as an open field. Thierry went outside for air while I chased my nephews with a fly fishing pole, dragging the crib box behind me.

We returned to the farm completely depleted. I microwaved some frozen mac and cheese while Thierry attempted to tidy his hair with gels and grooming cream. The phone rang; it was my mother. "Well, it's a girl! Why don't you drive the boys into town so they can meet their sister." It was either spike Thierry in the chest with the antique pitchfork that hung on the wall or get back in the car. It was a toss-up, but we all piled into the Bronco. This time I joined my nephews in the symphony of farts.

"This was not at all what I expected," Thierry

muttered under his breath. What had he expected, Camp David?

We were ten minutes from the hospital when my youngest nephew provided the grand finale to Thierry's big white-trash adventure: he shat his pants. I was not a mother and so didn't travel with wipes and hand sanitizer. I had lip gloss and an empty bottle of Xanax in my purse. I screeched the car to a halt and climbed into the back seat. I ripped off his Baby Gap jeans and underoos and threw them out the window onto the highway. I grabbed a Navajo blanket from the car floor and wrapped it around his waist. "We'll get you some pants in town. If you feel like pooping again, please stick your butt out the window." The boy was wailing, I was nauseous, and the stench overpowered the scent of Thierry's lime blossom facial oil.

My mother met us at the hospital front and collected the little boys, carrying the pooper in her arms like an old Persian rug. As they disappeared into the sliding doors of the emergency room, I turned to Thierry. "Maybe we should get balloons or something?"

He hit the side of the truck. "[*Strong French accent*] Are you joking? I want to get the hell out of here!"

"Fine," I said, attempting to defuse the situation, "let's go say good-bye at least." I had no intention of going anywhere, but the public display was embarrassing. Yes, I had just thrown a pair of underwear full of poo out the car window, but I still had a sense of decorum.

My sister's room was crammed with family members and friends. There was singing and streamers and bouquets of pink carnations. And then it happened. I watched it in slow motion. My mother poured Thierry's bottle of Dom Pérignon into Styrofoam cups and started passing them around the room—the champagne that was to signify the joy of our impending nuptials casually dispensed to random male nurses. Thierry stormed out of the room. And out of my life.

Au revoir, Thierry, but remember, we'll always have Kmart.

CHAPTER FIFTEEN

elevator down

The only perk of a meltdown is weight loss. At the peak of my valley I was ninety pounds. My skeletal body lay on the couch like a bundle of sticks as I blankly watched the World Cup. My best friend, Michelle, would drive by before work to bring me a Jamba Juice full of energy boosts. What I really needed was a metaphysical boost. If it weren't for my dog, I would never have seen sunlight or smelled air; even pouring dry dog food into a bowl was a Herculean chore. It was 1999; I had left my fiancé, my boyfriend of eight years, and my home, and was questioning everything about my life. And the human condition.

After a second week of insomnia and subsisting on stomach acid, my family descended on my *Bell Jar* by the beach. My mother was hoping that English muffins with sliced tomatoes would snap me out of it. And whenever I started to weep uncontrollably, someone would slip a Scrabble board under my chin. Maybe a triple word score would abolish any dark thoughts!

It was my brother who recognized that my dwindling

body fat and self-worth were not symptoms of a breakup, but something more psychologically rooted. It was the first time I wasn't dependent on parents or a boyfriend. It was just me. And I was anxious and scared. The little girl in me whose parents split just after I was born didn't want to be abandoned again. Yes, even though I had left my boyfriend. It was a moment in my life that plenty of vitamins and a brisk constitutional weren't going to fix. It was time to seek professional help.

The first shrink I saw had an office in a bungalow in Venice, California. The furniture was all petrified wood, and the plants grew out of avocado pits and cascaded down to the burnt sienna shag carpeting. I sat on a mushroom stool in the waiting room scanning the spines of books like *Tantric Love* and *Connecting to Your Orgasm* in the bookcase. Everything was breathing, bodies, and being. The therapist entered the room, a homunculus woman with a unibrow and a derriere the size of Kansas. She led me into her office and got straight down to business. "As we work together, I don't want you to be startled or ashamed, but you will find yourself having sexual fantasies and dreams about me."

I could barely swallow. "I'm sorry, sexual fantasies about YOU?"

She nodded. "You see, we will be forming a very intimate bond, and it's perfectly natural for you to sexualize it."

I stood up and walked out. I wasn't THAT fucked up.

I needed help, but I was in Hollywood, so actually finding a doctor who wouldn't rather be doing open-mike night at the Comedy Store or writing self-help books that would eventually star Ben Affleck was a challenge.

Next came a psychotherapist who would have been better suited as a network executive. She wore fitted pin-stripes and stiletto black suede boots, had flat-ironed hair and just a whiff of plastic surgery. Her saccharine earnestness came from listening to too many Marianne Williamson tapes. When she wasn't running her fingers through overly processed copper hair, she was pulling tiny pieces of lint off her Wolford stockings. Exhausted, I decided to stick my toe in her psych pool. One afternoon I succumbed to my unearthed vulnerability and cried. As I was describing the scene of watching my father pull away in the car, the "therapist" stopped me. "I'm sorry, where did you get those shoes?"

I took a beat and sniffled. "What?"

She moved closer, her eyes still on my feet. "I've been looking for those shoes . . . Barneys?"

I sprinted in my ballet flats right out of her office. I was now logging therapy sessions at ten-minute intervals.

My brother took me to a psychopharmacologist in Santa Monica who had been recommended by an alcoholic, unemployed actor friend of his, which at that point was good enough for me. The doctor's office was littered with New Guinean masks and whittled Indonesian sculptures of men with engorged penises. After forty-five minutes he handed me prescriptions for Xanax, Lorazepam, and Klonopin, and told me I needed to visit him at least four times a week. I mean, that panoramic view of Malibu wasn't going to pay for itself!

My brother filled the prescriptions, and I popped them like Milk Duds at the movies. This doctor had overprescribed me—my dosage would have sedated a tribe of elephants. In other words, I was higher than Keith Richards. I remember not being able to swallow water; it would dribble down my lower lip. I was also convinced that the chairs in my living room had wings. I stayed stationary on the kitchen floor, moving only to pee or sit up when Michelle brought me a shake. She would hold my head up like a paraplegic and pour the "mango-a-go-go" smoothie down my shirt.

Finally I flew to New York to seek a team of specialists. If you want your boobs fixed, you go to L.A. If you want your head fixed, you go to New York.

My mother traveled to New York with me, and we stayed in my little sister's one-bedroom Greenwich Village apartment. I hid under a mass of pillows in my sister's bed while she froze on her rickety couch in the next room. I played Scrabble with myself, and lost, while my mother whispered in the other room on endless secretive phone calls. One afternoon I heard her say "Silver Hill," which caused me to jump to my feet, hit the board, and send the letter tiles flying. Silver Hill is a psychiatric hospital in Connecticut. And I was damned if I was going to end up like Frances Farmer in a Lilly Pulitzer tennis skirt. "Mom, I am dealing with difficult life issues, I'm distraught, but I'm not trying to eat my own fist!" I guess it's a generational thing; in her day, you showed a little crazy and were shackled down on rubber sheets. In my generation, you show a little crazy, you get some books on incest and do a beet cleanse.

A friend told me about the outpatient program for anxiety and depression at New York–Presbyterian Hospital. It was day care for sad people. The first morning we sat in a circle in metal foldout chairs. There were eight of us— old, young, black, white, gay, and straight—holding coffee cups or peeling labels off bottled water. One by one patients would describe what had caused them to leave their families, work, minds, to be part of the group morning show. One woman went into harrowing detail about her husband's suicide, her children's removal to foster care, her near homelessness and addiction to Ritalin. The next patient was a young African American woman with gruesome scarification from years of cutting. Next was a man who was addicted to plastic surgery.

He had every implant invented, including abs, calves, and biceps—a man who wanted so much to be beautiful and yet fashioned himself into a grotesque freak. Whenever he ran out of money for surgery, he attempted suicide, so family members kept subsidizing his addiction.

One unfathomable story after another. Then it was my turn. I reluctantly stood up and cleared my throat. "Um. I was engaged to this guy, and I broke up with him. And then he took this really sexy actress to the Bahamas on a private plane." I quickly sat down again. The group looked at me like I had just strangled a puppy. Nobody said a word. The silence was deafening. Then the woman next to me put her hand on my thigh. Then the whole group hugged me. They all knew real pain, but didn't minimize mine. Although you know I'd be the first voted off the island.

We were in individual and group therapy from nine in the morning until five in the afternoon, with an hour free for lunch. The majority ate a Subway sandwich on a bench in the lobby or chain-smoked outside. I met my mother every day at the Plaza. It was right across the park. We would quietly sit in the Palm Court restaurant sipping split pea soup.

"How was class?" she would ask.

"It's called group."

"How was group?"

How could I possibly describe the heartache and pain these people were experiencing without trivializing it? "Fine." I knew my mother just wanted me to be back to normal, for the whole episode to be behind us. So we would quietly finish our iced tea, and I'd walk back to the hospital.

During this period the doctors started me on Zoloft—a drug I would invest all my money in, and practically do. I considered naming my first child Zoloft; it sounded Greek. Suddenly I had a floor. And the darkness was lifted. I felt like myself, for better or worse. I had periods of nausea while my body was adjusting to the medication. My mother and I would take leisurely walks up Madison Avenue, and I would stop to vomit next to a tree or in a trash can. My mother would rub my back like she was burping a baby. She wasn't embarrassed or humiliated by my actions; in her true style, she held her head high and acted as though everyone had a daughter circling the drain. Instead of it being the terrible twos, it was the terrible twenties.

By the end of the month I felt like myself again, or at least a stronger version of who I had been the last couple months. Maybe it was the drugs, maybe it was the realization that life could go on and that I could control it. Or maybe I saw what real pain and suffering was and, for the first time, felt extremely lucky and blessed. I hugged my support group good-bye. They still seemed perplexed about why I was there in the first place. Who knows, maybe a week at the Golden Door would have done the trick?

CHAPTER SIXTEEN

home box office

I had a farm in Africa . . . no, sorry, that was Meryl Streep. I had a Mediterranean-style three-bedroom in Los Angeles. This was post the Santa Monica hippie breakdown house. I had taken out a loan from my mother and stepfather, which I had vowed never to do because of the psychological strings attached. But that was before the sub-prime mortgage bonanza; California banks weren't yet knocking down the door to do business with every unemployed actress with a couple of script ideas at Paramount. My mother has always told me to have a little money saved in a private account, and ownership of some land or real estate. She knew too many women whose husbands ran off with their savings (and their assistants) or who never bothered to check invoices from their accountants and business managers. So she granted me the ability to own my first property.

The view behind the pool and the master bath were so spectacular I would have done mop-up at a slaughterhouse for the rest of my life to live there. It was up a private dead-end road high in the hills above Sunset Boulevard, which boasted a dramatic view of Century City (the corporate—not green—part of Los Angeles, so lots of lights all night). There were avocado trees, two orange trees, and a lemon tree. And fuchsia and purple bougainvillea that poured over the roof and cascaded down all sides of the house. And there was a pool, the one thing that separated the out-of-work actors who lived in their cars and the wealthy producers who slept with them.

I decided that instead of hiring a contractor who gave his workers a nickel to his dollar, I would erase the middleman and go straight to the artisans themselves. I have always been a supporter of the workmen that hang outside the paint stores or train stations. The many I have hired and befriended have shared with me extraordinary stories about escaping war-torn nations where they were dictators or mega pop stars, only to be reduced to begging for minimum wage and installing pet doors in this country. (Imagine Justin Bieber laying down miles of sewage pipe in the Ecuadorian desert.) I found a group of Mexican craftsmen who built, painted, and tiled an unzoned guesthouse for me. I found this entourage loitering in front of a Home Depot in East L.A.—a more optimal place for networking than AA.

I showed Luis, my right-hand man in the operation, a photo from *Elle Décor* of a guesthouse in southern France, and he erected it in a few weeks, complete with wooden beams and faux cracked walls. A safety hazard? Maybe, but when you lay down in the four-poster bed and looked out the windows onto magnificent cypress trees, it felt like *A Year in Provence*, so screw inspections and potential electrical fires. Plus, I lived up the road from a famous rapper who housed albino tigers and a rare snake sanctuary, and no city officials ever bothered him.

Every morning I would have breakfast laid out for me and my fellow carpenters. I made omelets to order, bacon, fresh orange juice from my tree, and coffee. Luis and I started to get really *Extreme Makeover: Home Edition*, and built an outdoor fireplace, a smokehouse (for meats and fish), and a vegetable garden with stone steps that led nowhere. I was Anthropologie to his Restoration Hardware. If everything we built hadn't been completely off the books, you'd be browsing our Web site today.

A round that time, my younger brother Tom, the eldest son from my father's second marriage, called and asked if he could come to L.A. for the weekend. He was looking for film work and figuring out next steps. Standard stuff. He arrived late on a Friday night and, instead of leaving Sunday afternoon, left a year from that Sunday afternoon. (He would have stayed longer, but I sold the house, and the new owners refused to Kato Kaelin my brother in the guesthouse.) Then my friend Lyle, a homophobic gay trainer in L.A., needed a place to stay for a week, which too stretched out until the sale of the house a year later. Lyle was from a southern town where he had been star quarterback and prom king. When his Republican parents got wind that his roommate, a black drag queen, might be gay, Lyle had to move out to protect his own life on the down-low. My home was becoming a halfway house of West Elm pillows and internal angst.

And then there was Kyra. Kyra was a friend from college who was statuesque and aimless. Every other week she changed her desired profession and moved to wherever there was a vacant rollout bed. She carted around mildewy tapestries, which she would drape over lamps, tons of beaded scraps, and flattering photographs of herself in various tropical settings. She was constantly in love either with someone who was married or someone who hit her; male, female, didn't matter. Kyra smelled like patchouli oil and glued in her own hair extensions. She called one morning to say she had a layover in L.A. for six hours, and could she come to my place for a quick drink. She had been living in Mazatlan, Mexico, but the wife of a guy she was seeing found out about her and burned down her place. The wife chased her down a dirt road waving a combat knife. Kyra was en route to White Plains to stay with her mother, a cognitive therapist, who was helpful to everyone she treated except Kyra. So she came up for a drink, fontina cheese, and rye crackers, and ended up staying in my home six months.

My solitary paradise was suddenly filled with my crestfallen chain-smoking brother, a trainer who ate broiled halibut for breakfast—my house smelled like a fish market during a heatwave—and an emotionally needy vagabond with daddy issues. I bought the groceries, paid the bills, cooked the food, did the laundry, and maintained the home in pristine condition. I was Mrs. Doubtfire without an interesting backstory. But I liked the whirlwind of my house. When people weren't crawling all over it leaving dirty boxers and hair in the sinks, I had dinner parties, and we played cards and jumped in the pool fully clothed. It had all the fun of the 1970s, but all the caution of the '90s.

My brother and I were in similar psychological states. He had also ended a relationship and was past the shaking it up phase and was looking to lay it down. I was no longer circling the drain, but doing my best to pull myself up to the porcelain rim. We spent many nights playing Trivial Pursuit and lighting one cigarette off the next. When he broke down and threatened to call every woman he'd ever met, I pulled the phone out of the wall. When I wanted to drive to my ex-boyfriend's house and steal his garbage, he would throw my car keys into the bushes. One night he misunderstood and threw away my keys when I simply wanted to go buy laundry detergent. We stank for days. He and I were both in therapy.

Tom had a rigid shrink. I had a strict Freudian woman who earned every penny. Every afternoon Tom and I shared the self-reflection of the day from our journals, things like his "I only love cigarettes" and my "I would choose pills over razors." Even though our shrinks were our emotional mechanics, we were always tinkering under the hood.

Tom tried to like other girls, but there was always "something." They had a mustache or chewed too loud or smelled like rancid pork. But the real problem was, he secretly compared every woman to Marisa Tomei.

⁓

Just when I thought my life would be reduced to dating assistant talent agents and herpetic actors, Dax entered my life. He was a British bad boy preparing to star in a big Hollywood movie. He was a strapping six-three, with great teeth (they were veneers, he's a Brit) and muscles just above his buttocks that sank in like little soup bowls. He was the man not every mother warned you about, but mine certainly did.

He was looking to rent a house, apartment; or room for six months while he was working in America. My friend Michelle, who partnered with his agent, called to ask if I was renting the guesthouse.

It had never occurred to me, plus I would have to move my brother to the guest room, the trainer to the library, and Kyra to the couch. I couldn't bear having to walk past Kyra and whatever gold-toothed imbecile she'd picked up outside the Olive Garden the night before. But Michelle pleaded with me to at least meet him.

The doorbell rang, and I, in my stunning wardrobe of PJ bottoms, a tank top, and hair pulled into a messy knot, opened it slowly and with slight annoyance. Shabang! It was instant primal attraction, on my part anyway. In a flash I excused myself briefly to slap on a pair of tight Levi's and cream blush. I giggled like a preteen and did my best sexy walk as I showed off the guesthouse and grounds.

"Well," he said, heading to the front door, "[*Strong British accent*] Not sure it's for me. I'm playing a Sid Vicious type character, and I'm afraid I'll be rather loud while rehearsing—"

"That's okay! That's great, not a fan of quiet," I interrupted.

"How much is it a month?"

"A hundred dollars," I said.

There was a long pause. "What?" he asked, clearly as dumbfounded as I was about my price.

"It's a hundred dollars because I'm picky about who lives here, and you are friends with Michelle." I was weak, desperate, and very attracted.

He sped away in a black generic sports car from

Hertz. He wanted to think about it. Shit, I should have said it was free.

Dax started filming, and I started doing his laundry. I prided myself on being the sexiest landlady for at least two miles (it was L.A., after all). One evening we found ourselves alone in the house, a rarity. He had never seen the movie *Shampoo*, which I explained was imperative for his cinematic education. During the opening credits we were already kissing. And by the next morning . . . Let's just say Warren Beatty and Julie Christie had nothing on us.

I consider this period of my life one of the great acting jobs. When Dax was on set, I would work on a script or putter around the house adjusting pillow placements or alphabetizing bookshelves. An hour before I guessed he would come home, I would shower, lather, exfoliate, tweeze, oil, moisturize, condition, spray, powder, and bleach. I would recline on the sofa in skinny jeans and a revealing white James Perse T-shirt and read *U.S. News and World Report*. I pretended to be cooler than I really was, younger than I really was, and more sexual than I've ever been. I created this character of the perfect woman. A woman who was never jealous, never nagged, and was addicted to semen. There were nights when he said he'd be home at 7:00 p.m. Those were the nights when I would sit there, covered in Jo Malone Nectarine Blossom &

Honey body lotion, with a plate of oysters and iced Cristal in front of the fire until the oysters looked like dried phlegm, the fire died, and the opened champagne was poured down the toilet. It was breakfast time.

I acted like I didn't notice he never came home. I said I was at a party in Malibu (or Manhattan, Miami, or wherever the closest city with male models was) and hadn't gotten back until 3:00 a.m. myself. "It was a nude, ecstasy orgy at Jake Gyllenhaal's, and I was the only girl." And he'd just stumble off to the shower. I could do without respect, gifts, compliments, faithfulness, orgasms, financial equality, or random acts of kindness. My whole self-esteem was dictated by the need to get this man to want me. Well, the pretend me. Let's call her Alice. I had been alone for a while and it was time to couple up again.

Six months into the torrid affair between Dax and Alice, he had to return to London. The weekend before he left, my mother came to visit. Thank God she stayed with an old friend in Pasadena, otherwise she would have witnessed Alice, her courtesan daughter, warming up hand towels, pouring tea, and sprinkling rose petals in his shoes. I could tell my mother found Dax entertaining; he was classically trained and could break into a whimsical Puck from *A Midsummer Night's Dream* at the drop of a hat. And it was during this week that I missed my period. I was convinced I was pregnant with a baby Jude Law. I was lying in bed watching *Guiding Light* when my mother came and sat next to me. "What's going on?" she asked.

"I think I'm pregnant," I answered, holding back tears. And fearing her damnation.

My mother took a deep breath, raised her eyebrows, and said, "Well, at least you know you can!"

My period arrived a few days later. Perhaps the stress of having my rarely sober, philandering boyfriend and my highly opinionated and intimidating mother together in the same room caused the biological blip.

When Dax's film wrapped, so did our relationship. Rather than go through the motions of a flaccid long-distance affair, we made a clean break. He flew back to London, where barrels of dark ale and seductive wenches awaited. And I went back to the PJ bottoms, tank tops, and disheveled hair.

———— ⌘ ————

Years later I married a man who gave me all that was deficient from the above, and Alice had finally vanished down the rabbit hole for good. Grey Gardens Two, as I had named my house, was a distant memory, my entourage spread far and wide. My brother married a sane and gorgeous girl, the trainer became a powerful (closeted) real estate agent, and Kyra changed her name, moved to Santa Fe, and sells dry ice.

My husband and I were living in Washington,

D.C., far from Beverly Hills. Our life was a series of dinners with journalists debating deficits and nuclear proliferation over cheese soufflé and artichokes vinaigrette. I would hear fleeting bits about what Dax was up to from the *Hollywood Reporter*. A Molière play here, a zombie movie there. Just scraping his nails on the roof of fame. I heard he was starring in a TV crime show, playing a hard-ass cop from Baltimore.

It was late afternoon, and I was holding my six-month-old daughter, singing that song about monkeys jumping on beds (which always struck me as slightly disturbing, because after they fall off the bed, they smack their heads. And by the way, why are lullabies so violent? When the bough breaks, the baby will fall? I don't know why she swallowed a fly; I guess she'll die?). The phone rang, and it was my agent. Apparently the aforementioned TV crime show was looking for a love interest for their lead, the inner-city cop played by Dax. There would be nudity. Ahem, n-u-d-i-t-y! They wanted me naked? I didn't have the kind of career that needed nudity clauses, R ratings, or nipple tape. The only time I did anything with even a whiff of a romantic lead to it was kissing Jerry Seinfeld (I was Schmoopie) in the infamous Soup Nazi episode. And even then, nobody wanted a second take.

I don't believe in astrology, but if I did, the universe had just pulled out an enormous rubber chicken. I laughingly explained to my agent that this job was inconceivable (so to speak) because he was an ex-lover, and that the last time I saw him he was boarding a Virgin Atlantic flight while I clung to his boots and screamed, "You don't know it, but you love me! You're in love with me, asshole!"

Two diaper changes later, my mother called. "You want to hear something funny?" I said.

"I don't know," she answered.

"I just got a call from my agent. Do you know the show called *The Beat* on HBO?"

"The violent show?" she asked.

"Yes, the violent show."

"I can't understand it."

"Well, nobody can, but they are interested in me for a leading lady part."

She responded without hesitation, "So do it!"

"It's not that simple. They are interested in me playing the love interest to Dax. Dax is the lead."

"Well, you should do it!" she repeated.

I took a deep breath. "Dax, who I used to be in love with! Dax, the playboy of the Western world? The one you said to have as an hors d'oeuvre and not the main course?"

"Well, there are not a lot of acting opportunities in D.C."

"Mom, let me tell you what the reality of this situation would be. It's five a.m.; I hand off your granddaughter to a nice South American woman I barely know who could steal or eat the baby, then get in a town car and drive two hours to the set. After hours of body makeup—because I'll be NAKED—I get on set and roll around with Dax for four hours in front of three cameras and God knows how many cameramen, kissing, caressing, and hopefully just dry humping. Then they call lunch, and because I am so confused and distressed, I go to Dax's trailer to talk to him. We end up making love all through break. I drive home hysterically crying in my town car because I can't shake the image of being thrown up against his trailer wall and knowing if I go back to the set, back to his arms, I might never leave again. Then what? I walk in the door, tell Lupe she can go home, and make a roast chicken?"

There was another extended pause. "Well," my mother finally said, "it *is* HBO."

CHAPTER SEVENTEEN

like a good melon, you know

I met my future husband in the restaurant of Barneys New York on a sublime spring afternoon. He requested dinner, I countered with coffee, we settled on lunch. It was my first blind date, and I didn't possess much faith in the outcome. I showered, but didn't shave my legs. I may have plucked my eyebrows, but I didn't bother with any makeup, not even Chapstick. I figured the date would yield an intriguing dinner-party story, nothing more. I had grown up in a family of political journalists, I had no interest in political journalism, and he was a political journalist—a very nice political journalist, I was sure, but a political journalist nonetheless. I assumed I'd become Mrs. Hugh Grant and live a Hollywood life split between our glass Gehry house in Malibu, our limestone flat in Notting Hill, and our tree house high in the banana plants of Barbados. Well, ultimately I knew that wasn't really my destiny; I knew tree houses had appalling septic systems, I was not a black transgender hooker, and I can only take so much brooding. The point is, I assumed I'd at least marry someone who was a member of AFTRA or SAG. Barneys New York seemed an ideal choice for lunch, because if the date ended up being social root canal, at least I could race upstairs and buy my Kiehl's grapefruit shower gel, and the day wouldn't be a total wash.

When George and I saw each other, we each did the perfunctory nod as if to say, "Ah yes, it's me, here we go, please work out." We shook hands and were escorted to a middle table—or, as I like to refer to it, theater in the round. We both ordered crab salad, which I didn't take as a sign; we both just like crab salad. I can't explain what it is that creates chemistry between two people. How many times have we asked ourselves, Why is he with HER? or, Why is she with HIM? I'm talking beyond the blatant he's-very-rich and she-has-very-large-breasts currency. When I met George, it was like coming home. There was a comfort and understanding. And, like you know when you tap and sniff a good melon, I knew. By the end of lunch we could have taken the subway downtown to the courthouse and exchanged I do's; it wouldn't have seemed impulsive.

I didn't play hard to get, but harder not to get. I was staying with my best friend Holly, who was a disciple of *The Rules* and urged me to act insolent, aloof, and unavailable. I didn't understand how one moved the relationship forward by being inaccessible. And I was too old for games. He would eventually see my cellulite anyway, so why bother with the Spanx? But Holly had a theory that involved pulling in big fish and teasing the worm and all kinds of confusing meta-phors. She had set me up with a man the week before (which was technically my first blind date, but I don't count it because I have done my best to repress it). She pitched him as a worldly Brazilian artist, so natu-rally I pictured a shirtless Benjamin Bratt splattered in oil paint. I sat at a table in the corner of Balthazar consuming a whole basket of bread and straining for a glimpse of every newcomer that walked in. And then a sixty-year-old gnome with a face smeared in orange self-tan, sporting a tweed foxhunting jacket, pulled up the adjoining chair—a pompous and insipid man who drove me to pick at my thumb so mindlessly, I had to excuse myself, run to the bathroom, and get a mound of Kleenex to staunch the bleeding. When the check came, I felt salvation was near. If he had gone for the brandy and cigar, I would have swallowed my own tongue. He offered me a ride in his white Hummer limousine, a vision of subtlety and elegance complete with light-up bar and candy dishes brimming with Altoids and condoms. When he threw himself on me and I coughed rape, he held the back of his hand up to my cheek and yelled, "Baste." I jumped out of the car. Sometimes public transportation is the safest way to travel, and I would have welcomed a brutal mugging over ten more blocks with that sociopath.

And that is why I consider George my official first blind date. The following day, he called for a second date. As I held the phone, Holly gestured around me like an overly caffeinated air traffic controller, whispering things like, "Say no, you're busy," and, "Tell him you'll see if you can get out of your date with Prince Albert of Monaco." Instead, I opted for full disclosure: "Yes, I'm free tonight and tomorrow night, absolutely no plans." Holly smacked her forehead and fell back on the couch.

George and I held hands and stared into each other's eyes, barely escaping oncoming cars and smacking into parking meters. We went to cafés and movies, forgetting to order or follow the plot. And after three days, just when we were heating up to the point of combustion, I was whisked off to a spa with my older sister and mother.

We had planned it months earlier, a bonding weekend for the girls and a chance to jump-start yet another healthy life plan. I had signed up for yoga, spinning, and a hot stone massage prior to the trip. I was going to shed pounds, steam out toxins, and find my third eye. I had not expected to fall in love— particularly not before a weekend at Canyon Ranch.

When I told my sister and mother about the date, they screamed. My sister was ecstatic; my mother fascinated but somewhat dubious—not about George, but about me. I spent the weekend on the phone chatting and chain-smoking, something health spas vigorously discourage. It's funny how in the beginning of the re-lationship you can spend two hours conversing about a cinnamon bun you had for breakfast, and then after a decade of marriage your conversations are summed up in quick transactions like, "Did you fix the toi-let?" My mother and sister would enter the room in leotards and sweatpants and leave freshly showered in cashmere scarves, with moisturized faces, off to sam-ple dairyless cheese soufflés and wheatgrass brownies. I don't remember eating, although my mother would bring back vegan bran muffins from the commissary and I know I was given a water bottle with my name on it at check-in. But by the end of our spa getaway, I was the one glowing.

George and I continued a cross-country courtship, he in New York and me in Los Angeles. And two months later we flew to Mykonos on our first vaca-tion. It would have been easier to have just gone to the Motel 6 in Paramus; we scarcely absorbed our sur-roundings as we clawed at each other like two kittens in a box. We stayed in a whitewashed stone hotel on the rocky cliffs overlooking the Aegean Sea. And as much as I enjoy looking out at the outlet mall parking lot, the teal ocean was a sexier backdrop. To detail the four days would only belittle the experience and read like a saccharine airport romance. Here's all you need to know: the view was breathtaking; I was with the right person, in the right place, and I was super thin. It's probably the only time in my life where I wore a bikini without a wrap and didn't get some form of dysentery from foreign cuisine.

The only non-Harlequin moment, aside from competitively sunbathing with George (a Mediterranean whose ancestors carried bricks up hills in the scorching sun), which resulted in me covered in painful blisters, involved an afternoon battle with hideous menstrual cramps. I swallowed a handful of Advil and passed out beneath the embroidered mesh net covering our bed in an ibuprofen coma. I was awakened several hours later by soft murmuring. "What?" I kept repeating. George was whispering in my ear. What was clear was, "I want you to be my wife." Instantaneously, the cramps subsided.

As cliché as it sounds, you do want to shout the news of your engagement from the rooftops, or cliff tops, or the Acropolis. If it were today, I would have texted, Facebooked, and Tweeted until dark. As it was 2001, we called George's parents, who were full of congratulations, then siblings, friends . . . and my mom. I detected a hint of caution in her response. Later I called Sissy. "What did Mom say to you about the engagement?"

She laughed. "Mom said when she sees you walking down the aisle, she'll believe it."

Okay, it was not the first time I had called with engagement news; at this point I had a box full of rejected rings. But this time around my mother would have to eat her cynicism with her Fiber Harmony over low-fat plain yogurt, because this union was going down.

CHAPTER EIGHTEEN

tied in knots

I had a big, fat, WASP Greek wedding, heavy on the Greek. What I didn't realize was, when you marry one Greek, you marry them all—approximately sixteen million. We were married by George's father, a priest, in a traditional ceremony in the Greek Orthodox Cathedral of the Holy Trinity on East Seventy-fourth Street. I walked in circles holding a candle amid a cloud of incense, promising loyalty and purifying my soul. I think. It was all Greek to me.

After we got engaged, I didn't have an industrial-size bulletin board overflowing with bridal dress sketches and wedding cake photos. I didn't become obsessed with picking bridesmaids or experimenting with a variety of hairdos with and without baby's breath. I had my two sisters stand with me, and I dressed them in dark brown polyester. And no accessories. They're very cute, so I had to take precautions; I was the bride, after all, I didn't need anything to steal focus. The only thing I weighed in on was the heart-shaped box made out of shells for the parting gifts. I just wanted to marry

George, and I was willing to endure all the shenanigans and circus acts that went with it.

My "Cindy Crawford barefoot on the beach in the Bahamas" wedding fantasy was instantly nixed, as was any form of elopement or destination wedding. George's father had presided over the most beautiful cathedral on the East Coast, so why make him stand shoeless on a reef in Eleuthera? It would have been like Vera Wang's daughter buying her wedding dress from Costco. With the venue set, I assumed we had all smoothly sailed over the biggest hurdle. (This is where the Greek chorus clutch their masks and gasp.)

George's mother is as formidable and strong-willed as mine. And I say that with admiration and respect. Both our mothers were dead set on the photographer they wanted, the people they had to invite, and how many troops it would take to invade Poland. The upside is, they're so much alike! The downside is, they're so much alike!

Weeks after the engagement was announced, my mother and I started scouting out potential venues for the reception. Naturally, as the bride, the reception was my prerogative, or so I thought. . . . We spent rainy New York afternoons touring limestone mansions with rooms for rent like the Metropolitan Club and the University Club. I would study my mother as she walked the spaces, daydreaming about the fete: twelve tables of ten, white roses and fresh lavender, cream linens, white asparagus in lemon dribble. "Mom!"

I would say as I elbowed her in her burgundy coat, breaking her trance. "There's only one bathroom, and it's two floors down—George has yia-yias, you know, Greek grandmothers, it's not going to work." And we would venture off to the next overpriced room that promised the most magical night of my life, with free mini quiches thrown in. In between appointments I was Googling "party lofts" and meatpacking boom-boom rooms. A little "yee-ha" for the yia-yias.

I have very little advice for people planning a wedding except for the following: do not go to tastings on an empty stomach. Also, don't use bronze body makeup with a white dress. I brought my mother to the acclaimed Sylvia Weinstock, the celebrated cake maker, for a sampling. Forkful of chocolate cake with buttercream frosting in my hand, I tapped the Limoges dish. "This is it. Delicious!" I instructed Ms. Weinstock to ice the cake light blue and decorate it with edible shells and sea life, and I would break up with George and marry the damn confection. My mother nibbled vanilla cake with lemon filling, chocolate and caramel, apricot, chocolate cake and chocolate mousse filling, hazelnut and key lime, and when I finally convinced her I had chosen the cake, she asked for a full slice of the chocolate cake with caramel filling. It was not really a tasting so much as a cake bender. My mother salivated about the chocolate cake for the next few days the way newly converted vegetarians fantasize about meat loaf. You would think after three weddings of her own,

these rituals would be monotonous, but she was as enthusiastic as a drunk girl during Fleet Week.

If it were up to my mother, the menu at my wedding
would have been that cake plus a shot glass of tomato
aspic. But that wouldn't fly with the Greeks. I had been
to a Greek wedding a few months earlier that boasted
culinary stations of the cross: a pasta, a moussaka, Chinese noodles, a meats station, cheese and salad, and so
on. This before the train of desserts. People don't realize that Greeks rival Jews when it comes to the buffet-
till-you-barf. I knew at my wedding we couldn't pass
around Triscuits and cheese and assume people would
drink their main course at the bar. WASPs don't feed
guests; they intoxicate them and then wait for someone
to call the Red Cross for doughnuts. I decided on filet
mignon and potatoes. The wedding was in November,
and a hearty meal seemed appropriate. Until I started
second-guessing myself. "What about people with al-
lergies?" I asked my mother.

"They can have cake!"

"And the vegans?"

She gave me that look. "Well, I assumed they
weren't invited."

The search for the perfect wedding dress is a ritual
that requires mandatory attendance on the part of the

bride's mother, mother-in-law, sisters, cousins, and any female she's met in her lifetime. The women are supposed to cry and hug when the perfect poufy dress is presented, and in the meantime eat Junior Mints and swig Diet Coke as they trade war stories about how men suck and they all cheat. I was on my way back from a Duane Reade run for Q-tips and hand sanitizer when I happened into Vera Wang's wedding dress store on Madison Avenue. I browsed one rack, saw a dress I liked, and bought it. I tried it on when I got home and figured I could take it to them for any tweaks. As an actress, nothing is as laborious or time-intensive as a costume fitting. The idea of trying on a million wedding dresses for one that wouldn't even make it into a major motion picture? What's the point? And that goes for makeup as well. Anything involving concealer and powder base is work to me. But I wasn't twenty-one when I got married, so the dewy, fresh, nubile look had to be contrived by a professional or a team of professionals. It took two full hours to make me look as if I were makeup-free. (A family friend sweetly asked a few days before my wedding, "Do you have time to get your eyes done?")

I was feeling on top of my wedding game but still didn't have a place for the reception. George called from work one afternoon. "We're having it in the church rectory."

I took a moment to let it sink in. "Um, but, I thought we could take a boat up . . ." The conversation ended there. It was his family's church. It was rude to have the ceremony in the church and then shuttle-bus everyone to another location. In November. Plus, I didn't want to lose any guests to the Italian joint down the street.

My mother met me outside the cathedral the next day. We both took a deep breath and entered the narthex. It's an awe-inspiring structure with a Mediterranean blue ceiling and a dome graced with gorgeous mosaics. We walked down the nave of the church to the altar, marveling at the beauty and the symbolism. My mother studied the sacrament table and the bishop's throne. "A lotta gold," she whispered.

"You can't change that, Mom." That said, she has never underestimated the power of a few well-placed ivy topiaries.

In this particular cathedral there was a man—more of a sprite, actually—who lived behind a hidden panel in the wall and would occasionally pop out and begin sweeping the floor with what appeared to be a makeshift Ethiopian fly swatter. When you made eye contact, he would evaporate into a mural of the Last Supper. On our first visit the little church man led my mother and me down the stone steps to the rectory. The room was pitch-black. There were no windows or light (I don't think Little Church Man had ever seen the sun) until he hit a switch and hundred-watt halogen lights, the kind your dermatologist uses to examine your moles, flooded the room. Now, I love my mother- and father-in-law, but this room, with stained linoleum floors and small stage, was designed for Sunday School assemblies and after-church coffee. Little Church Man showed us a couple of fold-out tables and an extension cord. All I needed for my nuptial extravaganza. Maybe I could conduct a few AA meetings between toasts. Before I could ask Little Church Man if we could cover up the school water fountain on the wall, he had vanished again. I looked to my mother, as I have at the onset of every major drama in my life. She took a moment. "It's going to take a lot of gauze, but I think we can do it."

Here's where the marrying one Greek means marrying them all. We wanted a hundred guests. My mother-in-law wanted a thousand. And that's a lot of spanakopita. But you can't have the Petropouli without inviting the Papadaki, who are related to the Kalfases whose son married Sophia Zorzos. And then there's the Pappases and the Callases, not to mention the Angelis, who live next to the Stephanideses . . . We decided my mother-in-law would throw her own engagement party. (You know the Greek chorus is gasping here too.)

The party took place a couple of weeks before the actual wedding. It was held in the church. In the same room as the reception. And, I believe, the entire population of Crete was there. I heard there was food, but I never even saw a discarded toothpick. George and I were standing like two Modigliani sculptures by the front door as a long procession of Hellenic folk pinched our cheeks and reassured George that he'd found a "nice one." And then the archbishop appeared, in cascading black robes. The archbishop is the Grand Poobah of Greek Orthodoxy, one step below their pope. We both kissed his ring, and we all gathered on one side of the room. All I know is he spoke for twenty minutes in Greek, and then he delivered a benediction. My mother-in-law got the wedding she wanted, and—if she's reading this right now—we *were* married that night, weren't we, Nikki?

———— ⌀ ————

Only a gay party planner with a knack for votives could transform that room into a wedding space fit for the royal family. And the design genius Robert Isabell was the man who did it. Not since I first saw *The Nutcracker* performed in a friend's basement, complete with snow machine and a real pony, had I witnessed such a transformation. I never had a bite of the food—although my mother told me the risotto balls were a hit—and managed only a couple sips of champagne. (As I had inherited my mother's inability to hold liquor, I felt my wedding reception was not the place to yank off my dress.) And we danced. The compromise had been a disco band to kick off the evening with songs like "We Are Family," and a Greek band to follow. The disco band lasted about half an hour before the Greek band muscled them off the stage. My favorite moment was watching my relatives try to Greek dance. It was like watching a group of old people auditioning for *Lord of the Dance.* Then mercifully they were swept up by George's family to snake around the room, screaming "Opa" at inappropriate moments. I reminded my stepfather not to hurl the china against the wall. Not that kind of Greek party.

George and I were dancing in a circle with our five-year-old flower girl. I still had cake crumbs on the corner of my mouth, and I was waving to an old friend I had promised the next dance. Suddenly my mother appeared and gently tapped my shoulder. "You have to leave now," she whispered.

"Why?" I swirled the little girl around, sending her orchid crown to the floor.

"It's almost midnight, and it's time for you to go."

I adjusted the crown. "Did the bar close?"

She gave me a stern look. "People want to go home, but nobody can leave until the bride and groom do."

I assumed I'd get kicked out of boarding school or book clubs I'd never attend, but kicked out of my own wedding? Thank God George left with me!

CHAPTER NINETEEN

there's no uterus like my uterus

Pregnancy. As soon as that pink stripe reveals itself, I am projectiling stomach bile like a dragon does fire. Some hormone allergy causes head spins and vomiting for six months non-stop. It's disgusting, maddening, and I feel like I'm losing my spleen through all the retching. Luckily, in my second pregnancy, I found a Web site devoted to a support group for people with hyperemesis gravidarum (Madmums. com). Yes, I have a disease, and the disease has a name.

I got pregnant the first time right after my honeymoon. I assumed it would take months and months to conceive, and we would end up pacing up and down the creaking planks of an orphanage in Athens searching for a Greek Oliver Twist. They still line up for you, right? My in-laws will tell you that there's never been a Greek boy in the history of adoption. The same way you would never find a Van Gogh at a yard sale.

Anyway, I was pregnant. I never had a day of craving BBQ spare ribs or waking my husband up in the middle of the night for shepherd's pie. Even an Arby's all-you-can-eat ribs commercial would send me dry-heaving off the furniture. It's important to note, we were married six months after meeting, pregnant soon after; the honeymoon phase was spent with my head in a toilet screaming, "Don't you fucking touch me!" One evening George came home to our little newly-wed apartment near Gramercy Park with a bunch of yellow tulips in his hand and a skip in his step. He was probably fantasizing us postcoital in white hotel robes sipping cognac in front of the fire, exclaiming, "Me too!" in unison at the end of each other's sentences. Instead, he walked in to find me stark naked in a pool of my own vomit in the middle of the living room rug. And to make matters worse, our two dogs were so revolted by my behavior it caused them to throw up. A whole Persian covered in sick. "Honey?" I lifted my head, still tethered to my own discharge of bile by a thick stream of drool. I know, why wasn't I ever on the cover of *Maxim*?

I was no better by my second trimester, just gaunter and more dehydrated. One of my most vivid memories is trying to shower with a bloody IV stuck in my arm and the metal IV stand, complete with drip chamber and plastic bag of saline fluid, in the tub with me. I'm sure George didn't second-guess leaving his life of bachelorhood filled with nubile cupcakes begging for a whiff of him for one minute! Okay, there weren't models throwing their panties at him at the news desk, but any pleasant, sensible gal would be more desirable than a shivering skeleton with a perpetual fur ball in her throat. In the ninth month, the illness subsided and I had a few weeks of normalcy until my water broke. And by normalcy I mean, I sat in a friend's pool in East Hampton devouring whole watermelons and crying uncontrollably and screaming (loudly, for all the neighbors to hear), "What happened to me?"

It doesn't matter how many DVDs of other peoples' births you watch (and never do that while eating lasagna, by the way), you are never prepared for labor. My mother was not forthcoming about menstruation, conception, and other "down there" issues, so labor was the most covert, terrifying experience imagin able. I still can't remember if I delivered vaginally or anally. The Queen or Kate Middleton should knight whoever invented the epidural. (And also the person who invented Skinny Cow ice-cream sandwiches.) I think the epidural should be administered just before consummation. Just keep a main line of numbing solution flowing throughout your system for months or even years. Why only for a few hours AFTER the pain has started? I see no harm, no foul, and I've never heard of a person checking into Promises Malibu for epidurals. Ah, a premenopausal girl can dream . . .

My water broke, I became hysterical, and George and I searched for the car keys. We never went to Lamaze or read books about labor—*What to Expect When You're Expecting* was like a Stephen King novel to me. When George and I went for the first ultrasound, the technician couldn't say definitively if our baby was a male or a female. The fetus's hands were covering the genital area. That's the WASP half. The nurse couldn't detect a penis. Somehow this translated to George's anxious mind that we were having a hermaphrodite. He was also reading the book *Middlesex* (about a hermaphrodite) and staying up late at night drinking too much roasted blend coffee and watching transgender documentaries. George was convinced I would give birth to a hermaphrodite. (Even after the baby was born, he kept grilling the nurse, "Does she have a penis? Does she have a penis?") Finally we entered the driveway of the hospital, and George started to look for a space in satellite parking level G9. "Go to the emergency room!" I yelled while imitating the way pregnant women breathe in the movies.

"Why? This isn't an emergency."

It's astonishing my husband was not castrated that evening. By this point I was white-knuckling the car door and his right arm—"When you go into labor, it IS an emergency, asshole!"

They placed me in a wheelchair, and a nurse who resembled Taye Diggs pushed me up to the maternity ward. I didn't want pressure on my buttocks. "Can't

I get on all fours on a gurney?" I had been vomiting in downward-facing dog position for close to a year and had become accustomed to that posture. The pain became so intense, I tried to convince the nurse I needed general anesthesia. I could be in a coma, have the baby, they'd clean me up, maybe blow out my hair, and wake me the next day? Ladies, why isn't this on our vision boards? Instead, an Asian man who looked like the maniacal, toothless bad guy wielding a syringe dripping with truth serum in every Schwarzenegger film entered my room with a rickety tray of potions and needles. After he'd poked me with the needle so many times you could connect the dots to form the Big Dipper, the epidural kicked in. All *namaste* in the world, and I was prepared to give birth for the entire island of Manhattan. Twenty minutes later two things happened: one, I gave birth to a six-pound nine-ounce fiery baby girl; and two, I decided men should pace in another room while women give birth, like they did in the 1950s. Nothing good can come from having one's husband witness a placenta the size of a down pillow and the color of flank steak come spewing out of one's vagina. And for the ladies that push a little too hard that they . . . how does that propel a marriage forward? My feeling is, Yes, you put the baby in, but if you can't get the baby out, go to the commissary.

My body had transformed into a warehouse abandoned of sexiness and incapable of seduction. I was once the bone at the dog races, and now I was a bloated mass of maxi pads and breast pumps. Labor ignites the minute you have contractions, and it never stops. You labor to produce milk, you labor to work off the fleshy accordion of a gut that will never experience a tan again, and you labor to stabilize hormones until you're hit with menopause. The only time a hospital stay is worth every insurance penny is when you've had a baby. There's no talk of death, buckets of blood, people crying while clutching rosary beads, or missing limbs. It's a happy ward full of balloons, pink carnations, and women walking like bow-legged cowboys as they make their hourly pilgrimage to the nursery. And if you forgo the creamed beef on toast and rice pudding and have a relative spring for take-out Chinese, it's close to nirvana. You sleep as much as you want, with no husband, kids, or barking dogs to wake you, and you have an epidural drip you administer whenever you want. Add a few Rob Lowe movies and a chocolate fountain and, seriously, why ever leave?

———— ✧ ————

My mother came to visit while I was in the hospital. This is the fundamental moment when a mother and daughter draw inspiration from their new roles as mother and grandmother. A time where only a mother can comfort a mother and dispense the intuitive wisdom passed down from generations of mothers. The only other experience that comes close is the preteen ear piercing at the local mall. My mother brought me trays of tuna salad and lemonade and reassured me that everything I was feeling was "perfectly normal." She would put the baby down on her stomach, and I would sneak back into the nursery and reposition her on her back. And she made the baby as unobtrusive as she could for my husband. My mother still subscribes to a world in which babies aren't meant to cause a man stress (the husbands need their sleep), and a woman breast-feeding in public is equivalent to a flasher on the subway. And my favorite, as I struggled with post-pregnancy bleeding, engorged mammary glands, and postpartum blues: "You know, it wouldn't hurt to fix your hair a little before George gets home from work."

After my first child, my mother dispensed her phi-losophy on a women's reproductive system: "Get it out."

"What?"

"Get a hysterectomy. It was the best thing I ever did."

"Mom, I don't want a hysterectomy, we want more kids."

And then my mother gave me the look she gives when she is very serious. Her lips get pursed, and her right eyebrow rises so high it almost joins the hairline. "Let me tell you something about your uterus."

"Um, okay?"

"When you get older, it becomes a huge, heavy sponge." I clutched my middle. "You remember our basset hound, Celeste? Remember how she used to drag her stomach on the floor? That's what happens!" Silly me: I had always assumed this was due to the fact that Celeste had six litters over the course of her life. And don't all parts of a basset hound drag a bit? Should I get my ears taken in?

I never had a hysterectomy. I've always felt possessive of my innards, and have never been clear on precisely what one does with the extracted ovaries. Have them bronzed and made into bookends? I rarely second-guess my decision, but every once in a blue moon when I'm at the dog park, I'll see an aged, paunchy beagle and think, "Oh lady, you should have had a hysterectomy."

well-mannered

My mother instilled in us exemplary ethics and manners: always, she taught us, be gracious, grateful, and good. We would have our thank-you note written and stamped before we even finished unwrapping the gift. In this age of global technology domination, we still hand-scribe our much-obliged sentiments on monogrammed stationery, as opposed to the toneless and detached e-mails that butcher gratitude with "thx" or the revolting LOL. I can't imagine Babe Paley or Diana Vreeland sending an OMG to Truman Capote the morning after the Black and White Ball. We were taught a basic rubric of appreciativeness: thank-you notes for dinners or event invites; a large bouquet of flowers if the dinner honored you; if the party was smaller than ten, a petite bouquet. Hostess gifts were as follows: if you were a guest for one night, linen hand towels or a set of seashell hand soaps; a weekend stay, something more deluxe like a case of wine or tortoiseshell salad tongs. Once we fully absorbed the etiquette manual, it became second nature, like flossing and changing underwear. Everyone in my family has personal stationery and says thank you whether we've received something or not and please whether we want something or not. My children panic about their birthday lists based on the sheer number of notes they'll have to write the next day; it's almost worth saying "no gifts," but even then they'll have to thank their friends for attending.

I had just moved back to Washington after nearly a twenty-five-year hiatus. I was not happy about relocating to a city where people barked like seals about Gallup polls. I left Los Angeles, the city of sycophancy to fame, for a city of sycophancy to power. After many years in Hollywood, my relationship with manners was rusty. It's a culture of thank-me, not thank-you. A place where you expressed your gratitude by allowing someone to take a percentage of your salary and were beholden to others only during awards season. Washington is not so blatant; there are politics dictating how you handle politics.

The first winter back in D.C., my husband and I were invited to Secretary of Defense Donald Rumsfeld's Christmas party. (Washington is a small town, and like in kindergarten, if you invite one person, you have to invite them all.) My mother has always said, "The chicest thing to wear when you're unsure is black pants, a black turtleneck, and black flats." My wardrobe at the time consisted of sparkling Hollywood mini dresses that made me look like one of Beyoncé's back-up dancers. Not knowing how to dress for a Republican holiday cocktail fete, I went with my mother's advice. It was beyond understated; all in black I looked like part of an off-Broadway tech crew.

The party was festive; senators were sipping hot buttered rum, and Condoleezza Rice was admiring my daughter's princess shoes from Target. I kept checking to see if Cheney was hoarding all the pigs in a blanket. All accompanied by a high-pitched yapping from downstairs. It was a familiar yelp in an unfamiliar place, so I inquired about it. "It's our dachshund Reggie, and we have a new puppy, Chester," Secretary of Defense Rumsfeld answered, beaming with pride. It was fascinating to think that the defense policy adviser who had declared a global war on terrorism was being guarded by a beast the size of a mango. He took me downstairs to meet his beloved sausages. Since I grew up with dachshunds and was an active member and recipient of the Dachshund Friendship Club newsletter (I have the dachshund snow globe, key chain, and stemware), I understood the extent of his allegiance to the breed. And there they were, in a basket with a Rudolph fleece throw in the laundry room. They were curled up like a gingerbread Bundt cake. The secretary of defense's face was uncharacteristically joyful as he helloooed his canine friends in a high-pitched voice, a voice I'm sure he never used during heated calls about Saddam

Hussein. We cooed and petted, and before Reggie was worked up into a tinkling frenzy, we returned to the party. As a silver tray of endive and Roquefort passed by, Rumsfeld confided, "You know, there's a great essay about dachshunds by E. B. White." I was only familiar with the children's book *Pretzel* and the barking hot dog named Waffles in the film *Manhattan*. I was excited to have another literary reference added to my dachshund repertoire. I thanked him, then followed a tray of chicken satay into the other room—again, to see if Cheney was hoarding all the pigs in a blanket. Assuming the hot dogs could actually be found in all the flaky pastry as Cheney was so sure they would be.

After an hour of pleasantries and many cocktail napkins filled with baked ham skins and shrimp tails, we decided to leave before our toddler melted down and spat hazelnut Yule log on Colin Powell's shoes. In the car ride I was pleased to conclude that there was very little difference between Democrat and Republican Christmas parties, with the possible exception of plaid blazers and a higher caliber of booze at the latter. And the irony that the man who declared the existence of Iraq's weapons of mass destruction adored the dogs bred to flush badgers out of holes.

I devoted the next morning to my routine errands, picking up a chicken and aromatic lavender bath salts at Whole Foods and Good Humor chocolate éclair ice-cream bars at Safeway. And the *Economist* (okay fine, *Us Weekly*) and Crest white strips from CVS. I had my pile of mail to send, including a cream Tiffany thank-you card for Secretary of Defense Donald Rumsfeld. As I passed Barnes & Noble, I recalled our conversation about E. B. White and quickly parked in front of a hydrant. I could hear my mother: "What a perfect, personal thank-you gesture." I quickly located the book, an Ina Garten cookbook for my husband, and the revised *Joy of Sex* (which I'm glad they revised, because the first one is still confusing). They gift-wrapped the E. B. White book in paper that featured tiny globes, which seemed apropos. It was that or baby jungle animals.

I drove a hybrid SUV that was sullied from a long winter of dirty snow and beaten up by my husband's novice navigational skills. He's one of those men who believe road rules don't apply to them. I once asked him how many times a day another driver gives him the finger, to which he answered, "Enough so that I take cabs." The trunk was filled with spilled groceries, there was a baby seat covered in mushed animal crackers, and an abundance of empty Starbucks cups were scattered on the floor. I wore my daily uniform of jeans, Tretorn sneakers, and a black down jacket.

And, as usual, no makeup and hair pulled back in a ratty knot. Always a before, rarely an after.

I pulled up in front of Secretary of Defense Rumsfeld's handsome brick mansion, which had an American flag hanging from the second-floor balcony. Keenly aware of the ice cream in the trunk, I grabbed the book and the card and skedaddled across the street. I assumed the secretary wouldn't be home; it was a workday, and we were, after all, at war. I didn't want to dally, exchanging pleasantries with a housekeeper or dachshund sitter. I contemplated ringing the buzzer at the side gate, but I've never been partial to screaming my name into a faceless battery-operated box. So I tucked the card inside the Barnes & Noble bag with the book and gently tossed it over the gate.

Within seconds I was surrounded. The gardener, the phone repair man, and two guys in sunglasses sitting in the black Suburban, all packing heat, circled me like we were about to play a mean game of Trust. I instantly threw my hands in the air, one of the many important things I've learned from television. "I'm just dropping off a gift! It's a gift! It's a book. It's an essay about a dachshund." I was stuttering like a guilty person. The two men in black snatched the package and sped off with it in the Suburban.

I found out later that the book was whisked to McLean, Virginia, to be inspected and X-rayed. I apologized profusely to the undercover agents and asked them to please go back to pruning the magnolia trees. Apparently, I was lucky; I wasn't strip-searched in the basement of the CIA or detained in a terrorist holding pen. How heinous would that have been? Don't forget, I had ice cream in the trunk.

When I tell people this story, they laugh uproariously at my stupidity and naïveté. Yet as preposterous as it was to throw a package over the gate of Secretary of Defense Rumsfeld's home during wartime, at least he received a handwritten note and a thoughtful and personal gift the next day. As Fred Astaire once said, "The hardest job kids face today is learning good manners without seeing any." I only wished my mother had been there to see it.

Perhaps if I asked politely, they might give me a copy of the security tape . . .

CHAPTER TWENTY-ONE

coming home

"E very time I try to get out they pull me back in," Al Pacino famously declares in *The Godfather*. I never knew a line from a violent movie about the clandestine empire of the Mafia would resonate so much in my own life. Everybody has feelings about their origins. How many times have I heard, "Well, that's 'cause I'm from the Midwest!" which is supposed to symbolize something, exactly what, I've never understood. You're amiable? Eat corn? What? It's easy to stereotype every upbringing based on the birthplace: Houston, Georgia, North Korea. . . . But not so easy with Washington, D.C. "You mean you're from Maryland?" "No, Washington." "Where in Virginia?" "Actually, Washington." "IN Washington?" "Yes, my mother gave birth on the steps of the Jefferson Memorial!" It's different if you work in D.C., it's a land of political opportunity. But to be born there? Nobody has a reference for that.

I was conceived in the Bahamas, but born in Washington. I often wondered if it were reversed, what kind of life I'd have. Well, conch fritters whenever I want. And skin cancer. The distinction in growing up in the nation's capital is you are being raised in the heart of all the machinations of government and politics. When I would go trick-or-treating in D.C., it wouldn't be startling to have Walter Mondale or Al Haig toss Milk Duds and Charleston Chews into my pumpkin bucket. It was always funny to me when I lived in L.A. and kids would ring the bell wearing Nixon masks because I actually got Snickers and Milky Ways from the real one. And we would toilet-paper people's houses regardless of their stand on *Roe vs. Wade*. Growing up, if a parent was late to watch a soccer game, it wasn't because the advertising pitch went late or they had trouble closing the shop early; it was because they were deciding whether or not to bomb the Soviet Union. "Sorry I was late for the gymnastics meet, but I had to sign the SALT treaty." Imagine trying to sell Girl Scout cookies to Oliver North? The majority of my friends' parents worked in government, and those who didn't relied on the people who worked in government to hire them. And we didn't really know the specifics of anybody's job: her father was a lobbyist, she worked in the State Department—beyond that, we had no idea. I still don't know what a lobbyist does.

I knew what I wanted to do by the time I was toilet-trained, and it wasn't working as Shriver's chief of staff. I was going to be Farrah Fawcett and have pool parties with Kristy McNichol and Mr. T over for tacos. D.C. was so boring. All anyone ever talked about was the headline of the *Washington Post*. And just the political and global news, never the entertainment section. I was at a dinner party for the new assistant secretary of state and nobody there knew JULIA ROBERTS HAD JUST GOTTEN MARRIED! Talk about ignorance!

Even when my stepfather was accused of being a spy under the Nixon administration, I took nothing seriously. The FBI had wiretapped our phones, which was daunting and intimidating to my siblings, but I discovered a new recreational pastime, intercepting conversations and yelling "Balls!" into the handset. The tapes now exist somewhere in the Library of Congress. My fifteen minutes.

When I finished college and moved to Los Angeles, I felt like I had finally claimed my life. I was exactly where I wanted to be, doing exactly what I wanted to do, waitressing and auditioning in abandoned warehouses for non-union soft porn. My view was not of the Kennedy Center and the Potomac River, but of palm trees and freeways clogged with assistant costume designers and key grips. I would live out my days in Hollywood and eventually be buried at the Forest Lawn cemetery next to Andy Gibb.

In 2002 I was knocked up and living back in D.C., a mile from where I grew up. Just how the hell did this happen? And I was married to someone who had a Sunday-morning political talk show. I felt like I'd been punk'd by the universe. As a child, my options were limited, but I was a grown woman! I could live in Palm Beach and raise polo ponies if I desired! Or reside in a nonreligious surf cult village in Kahoolawe! I had to scramble psychologically to make my version of D.C. a nonsuicidal endeavor. I called my old shrink for an emergency tune-up. It went to voice mail.

I found as an adult I was grappling with more than being at dinner parties where diplomats screamed over me about NATO probing and world market slips. I was now living in the town where, at my age, my mother had been the toast *de la ville*. And I don't mean because she had a powerful job as White House social secretary, although that was a significant perch, but because she was so revered and adored. And still is. When I started to immerse myself in Washington society, I was continually met with the same comment: "You are the spitting image of your mother!" Which would, undoubtedly, lead to millions of questions about how she was and what she was up to. Everyone knew her. And they were all her age. The people I had sung "Edelweiss" to in my nightgown as a child were now my dinner partners. This took a long time for me to wrap my head around. Some of these women were on committees and boards with my mother, and now they wanted to have lunch with me? I had to start calling them Lucy and not Mrs. Lawrence? And they were divulging intimate secrets to me? I didn't want to know what kind of geriatric sex the people who used to bounce me on their knee were having!

I made a private pact that I would be true to myself; I would dress, speak, and dance without inhibition. Somewhere between Martha Mitchell and Hanoi Jane. My acerbic and irreverent behavior liberated me from my mother's legacy. I discovered one evening, when I was seated next to Alan Greenspan (and I barely knew how to balance a checkbook), that anyone with a copious Wikipedia entry actually prefers to discuss anything but their vocation at social events. In fact, Mr. Greenspan loves jazz and really appreciates a good dirty joke. People in D.C. get exhausted from the pedantic inside-the-Beltway talk and want to know what a thruple is (a relationship consisting of three people) and what doing it "old school" means.

I was recently at the White House to emcee an event with First Lady Michelle Obama. When she came to the podium, she said, "I was just upstairs with the president, and he asked me who was emceeing my event. I said, Ali Wentworth, and Barack said, 'Really? She's very funny, but isn't she a little . . . inappropriate?' "

Well, there you go, I thought. I'm sure Reagan never called my mother inappropriate. And in my world that's a real compliment.

CHAPTER TWENTY-TWO

a big bowl of baby

When we started planning our eldest daughter's baptism, I envisioned a quick service, a blessing on the forehead followed by a brunch with eggs Florentine, mimosas, and silver vases of pink peonies. Baptisms, to me, were about holding up a baby, dressed like a Victorian doll, for photographs, and tables of Tiffany rattles and monogrammed hairbrushes. Not so for the Greeks.

My father-in-law presided over the service at the Saint Sophia Greek Orthodox Cathedral in D.C. All the Greeks (not quite the sixteen million) and WASPs (all twelve) were in attendance, both sides with very different expectations: the Greeks excited for the religious and cultural celebration, and the WASPs anxiously trying to remember if they were ever confirmed so they could claim their sip of the Communion wine. I didn't have any expectations of my own; I knew my father-in-law was the go-to guy for sacraments. Our large cast of familial characters had not been in the same room since the wedding, and I was relieved not to be the focus again.

There was no doubt that George was beloved and worshipped on my side of the family. The thought bubble over my mother's head the day of our wedding read, "How the hell did this happen?" He was so smart, sophisticated, handsome, and accomplished—I myself asked, "How the hell did this happen?" Well, sometimes these things can't be explained. As Woody Allen once said, "Nothing worth knowing can be understood with the mind. Everything really valuable has to enter you through a different opening." Not that any of my orifices are exemplary or better than others'. Sometimes I think if George and I were both drowning in a lake, my mother would, without hesitation, jump in and save him. Then he would remind her that I was still in the water, and they would collectively call someone for help.

As to what George's family thought of me? I had just six months earlier given birth to their first grandchild, which pretty much afforded me demigod status. Yes, my husband was a Rhodes Scholar, but could he incubate human life?

Any event involving family is all about coordination and hydration. The morning of the baptism was spent on the phone repeating the address of the

church, the time of the service, and what I was wearing. And then I would hang up. My daughter Elliott
was in a particularly feisty mood. I think she knew all
the cooing over her was not going to lead to a Wig-
gles concert. And stuffing her into my grandmother's
musty white christening dress left her sweaty and even
more irritable. Plus, I was holding her like a football
as I tried to shimmy into a skirt I wore before pregnancy. The fact that it was ripping at the seams and
I looked like a sausage didn't deter me. After Elliott
was born, I lost all sense of body image, meaning I
was in denial and assumed it looked the same as it did
when I was in college. To this day, I wouldn't know I
had cellulite, age spots, and gray hair if my kids didn't
point them out daily.

So here it was a year after the wedding, and we
were all back in a Greek Orthodox cathedral with the
Greeks on the right side and non-Greeks on the left.
Elliott was fidgeting in my arms, dressed like something you'd see on a float at the Puerto Rican Day
parade. The two of us struggled to keep the silk bonnet on her head; she would pull it off and I would
scotch-tape it back on.

At the beginning of the baptism, I was instructed to
lay the baby down on a white towel and disrobe her.
"Can she keep her bloomers on?" No. "Can I wrap
her in a blanket?" No. So I stripped my little girl down
to her nakedness, and she screamed like someone had
bitten off her foot. I'd never seen her turn purple.

Elliott was then anointed with holy oil. It was rubbed all over her skin like she was a Greek chicken. All she needed was a lemon shoved up her butt and a sprig of rosemary. Babies are supposed to enjoy massage, but I think Elliott knew she was being prepped for something. Like dinner. She wasn't going to get a bottle or her jingly caterpillar until she renounced Satan. I was told that because babies don't have the word capacity to renounce Satan, the godparents do it for them. The way her bloodcurdling screams echoed through the church, it was clear that the Devil seemed to have a tight grip.

My father-in-law held his grandchild in his arms and lovingly blessed her. Then he abruptly submerged her in a copper bowl full of water. When I say submerged, I don't mean a sprinkling of holy water on her forehead or a splash of water on her legs; I mean down in the diving bell at the bottom of the sea. When her purple face popped up, eyes closed, mouth open, and the piercing scream came, I thought she would take her tiny hand and slap the whole row of us. Then she was pushed back into the bowl again—not twice, but thrice. All I kept thinking was, "She'll remember this, and when she's a hormonal teenager she will shoot me point-blank in my sleep."

I looked out at the congregation. My in-laws and various Greek relatives and friends were gleefully smiling and snapping photos like we were in Disney World, happy times! Click click click.

Then I looked over at my mother. She was pale, and you would have thought by her expression she was watching the Khmer Rouge bite the heads off kittens. My sisters had their faces in their hands, and my brother was about to cry. The room was watching two different movies—*It's a Wonderful Life* and *The Texas Chain Saw Massacre*.

When the service was over and my baby was buttoned back into her christening dress, the whole congregation made their way over to our house for the party. And these two families melted together in hugs and cheers and toasts over a big buffet. Elliott was passed out in her stroller like a barmaid on New Year's Day, her bonnet tossed to the floor. People were sitting on the floor, on steps, outside, holding plates of meringue cake and flutes of bubbly. Everybody mixing, laughing, wondering what to do with the white-chocolate-covered almonds . . . (the Greeks give them out at every occasion). They may have all taken different roads, but everyone ended up in the same celebratory place in Elliott's honor. And to this day, when Elliott sees a pot of boiling water she locks herself in the coat closet.

CHAPTER TWENTY-THREE

i don't get
vacation

I hate family resorts. I'm happier in my own bed with a bowl of Honey Nut Cheerios watching the Travel Channel. It's not vacation if I can't sleep most of the time, hear the cacophony of car horns, and walk around naked without the entire building across from us laughing. Resort vacation is the same stress of everyday life, just in a nicer setting. And surrounded by the same people. We leave New York to get away from New Yorkers only to be trapped among New Yorkers, in fewer clothes. And who told the Germans in the room next to us it was okay to blare Japanese technopop at 4:00 a.m.? And the three-hundred-pound sunburned guy wearing a thong to keep buying us drinks called Sex on the Beach? As Lenny Bruce once said, "Miami is where neon goes to die." And the weather isn't always so reliable; I've spent five days on an island in the Turks and Caicos watching every episode of *My Wife and Kids* during a monsoon. After you've been to all the spots hailed by Expedia, they start to blend together. Did we dance to that steel band and eat grilled snapper in Antigua? Barbados? Or was that a fortieth birthday in Teaneck? We took the cruise from Puerto Vallarta? Or was it Greenland? The glass-bottomed boat, the dirty-talking parrot, the bottle of colored sand—I look at the photos and barely remember any of it. And as much as I hate resorts, I just keep going to them. I keep thinking the next resort will change my opinion. In a soufflé recipe one must gently fold in the egg whites; that's how I view my history of resort vacations, a softly blended pile of fluff. I didn't relish vacations as a child (sun poisoning), and it hasn't gotten better as an adult. My honeymoon was beyond perfect, but we didn't need to be in St. Barth's; we would have been happy locked in a kennel cage in our garage.

Every summer my husband and I take our two young daughters to Greece. We think it's important for them to be immersed in their religion and culture and to understand that many women have dark mustaches. We eat foods with tentacles and basically bathe in feta. Each day is a new adventure exploring beaches and their tavernas. You can have a four-star meal in your bathing suits there, and I will choose linguine with lobster over a Dora the Explorer popsicle from the parking-lot truck any day. We get very lax and follow painted cardboard signs and arrows with the word *thalassa* (the sea) nailed to cypress trees. One day last summer we found ourselves on a lovely crescent-shaped beach, sun beaming down, ocean the color of Ralph Fiennes's eyes . . . Oh, and packed with frolicking gay men. I took my four-year-old's hand—she was dressed in a red strawberry bikini and pigtails and holding a Kermit the Frog pail and shovel—as we took an ocean stroll. As we made our way through the cluster of perfect physiques with too much oil, she clocked a Filipino man dry-humping a peroxide-blond German with a My Little Pony tattoo and a cowboy hat. "Mommy, what are they doing?" Hmmm . . . excellent question. First of all, there's nothing wrong with what they were doing—I believe in gay marriage, gay rights, everything gay—but any two creatures, be it straight, gay, or amphibian, twisting tongues and flexing their buttocks shouldn't be on public display without a cover charge. "He's tickling him," I said, swiftly moving on. She was too young for full disclosure: I was too old for full disclosure. And so my afternoon was not filled with the usual drooling naps, sandy cups of lemonade, and search for twinkle shells. When I wasn't building a private cabana out of our towels and T-shirts, I was answering questions like, "Who's Ricky Martin?" and "What's transgendering?"

Recently we took the girls to the Bahamas for spring vacation—the week when children have no school and grown-ups do their jobs from BlackBerries, pretending they saw Scooter's cannonball into the pool and oohing over the sea-glass ashtray Suzy made at the kids' club. And let me add one thing about resort kids' clubs: just how thoroughly do they vet potential counselors? One New Year's Eve we left our daughter at a kids' club and were somewhat concerned, as the counselor had very red eyes and was "off." When we came back, she was passed out on the floor. Good thing the DVD of *Annie* automatically replayed. We have a friend whose little boy was expelled from a kids' club in Mexico; I was always afraid to ask, Just how does a toddler get expelled from a kids' club? Apparently it involved paintbrushes, turpentine, and peeing off the balcony.

So, we were in the Bahamas, and suddenly our younger daughter, Harper, came down with strep throat, with (based on an unpredictable magnet thermometer you press on the forehead) a 109-degree fever. We raced to the local island clinic in a rusty golf cart. It was a bubble gum pink building with broken windows surrounded by burned grass. The hospital consisted of a rickety chair, a roll of medical tape, and an illustrated guide to chlamydia. All three very helpful. The next few days I lay in a dark hotel room with just the rattling sound of the ceiling fan and crashing waves, holding my daughter's hand as she sweated and cried to get back to New York. In her feverish delirium she sounded like Martin Sheen in *Apocalypse Now*. Poor thing had to look out on an ocean she couldn't play in, smell fruit concoctions she couldn't digest, and swig penicillin that ended up in my hair. I can only hope it was penicillin; it was a thick white paste in an old bottle that pirates used to drink from in days of old. And worst of all, there was no SpongeBob SquarePants on the island. The yellow piece of cheese, or whatever he is, has gotten us through some very tough times. My eight-year-old had her hair bead-braided, which made her look like a Florida State student on spring break. But that's what you get when you leave your husband in charge in the tropics.

I split my time between bike riding with Elliott and pinning down a screaming and writhing Typhoid Mary as I poured liquid Tylenol down her neck. There would be an hour at two in the morning when I would roll over and spoon my husband. It was the moment that would reassure us that we loved each other and that this was all part of our journey together. Beyond that, our vacation interactions extended no further than hissed exchanges: "You go back to the room and get sunscreen, I've been up three times!" and "If you knew the grouper tartare was going to be disgusting, then why did you order it?"

Word got around the hotel that we had a feverish child, and suddenly I had moms in lime green Roberta Freymann kaftans approaching me in the restaurant. Coming to my rescue. "Listen, I have pow-dered Amoxicillin, Tylenol, Motrin, Pepto-Bismol, a Z pack, Benadryl, Neosporin, and Ritalin if you need it." I realized this is how vacation is with children. These women were generous, friendly, and prepared; they knew they had a fifty-fifty chance of getting a tan and reading the new Judith Krantz novel or sit-ting under an umbrella with a toddler hidden beneath towels, coughing up phlegm. And the more children you have, the more you up your odds. No matter how fast my golf cart went, I would never outrun the curse of the family vacation.

———— ⌥ ————

As I lay next to my moaning, feverish baby girl, I started remembering vacations we took when I was a child. Was there a lot of sickness? Did my mother have to go below deck and hold someone's hair back as they retched over the toilet? You never remem-ber those moments when you're a kid. You remem-ber long, boring car trips when you wanted to smash the window and roll out of the car that was packed with siblings, canines, and 7-Eleven detritus. Even my mother had moments where she had to descend to the filthy level of family vacation. When I was thirteen, we drove in a blizzard through Idaho, and my mother, in horror, realized there was nowhere but a tundra to relieve herself. There would be no aloe soap or Frette hand towels, just snowy brush and coyote skulls. My mother marched out about a hundred feet, pulled up her ankle-length black mink coat, and became one with a saguaro cactus. The rest of us held it in for the next six hours.

Then there were the beach vacations where I sat on a towel in the ferocious sun, wondering why people travel so far only to sweat and burn. And my older sister was always developing rashes or getting stung by some undersea monster. We all were endlessly covered in bites from sand flies, mosquitoes, and mites. And I knew if I had ever gotten a foot into the ocean, it would have been swiftly dismembered by a killer shark, so I never took the risk. Is my sharkophobia getting redundant?

Nothing was as awful as ski vacations, though. I honestly would have preferred a third-degree sunburn in Mexico. What was to like? Mummified in snow-suits with itchy long winter underwear, extra socks, hats, gloves, scarves, all to slide on two wooden sticks down a hill. What was particularly unnerving was not my inability to exit off the chairlift without falling, but being sent to ski school for most of the day. How did a week off from school spent in another school qualify as vacation? The parents were swigging red wine and gorging on cheese fondue as they waved at the suffering toddlers sliding down the icy mountain, snow-plowing so deeply their knees snapped.

My mother believed all the torture would be worth it if she gave me a pack of Wrigley's fruit gum. It did help with my frostbitten lips, but a Band-Aid for my cold abandonment? She would pull me to ski school, repeating affirmations like, "Just put your mind to it" and "Nothing is impossible." By the way, Mom, "Whoever said nothing is impossible never tried nailing Jell-O to a tree."

One morning I pleaded for a potty break but was told disrobing would take too much time; I would miss the beginning of my ski school class. My mother consequently had the embarrassing pleasure of watching steam surround me like a manhole in downtown New York as I was pulled up the T-bar, peeing all the way. Sissy performed the same act, and we were made to finish the class in soaked parkas and melted egos. It was on this same trip that a man (desperately in need of anger management) determined that my sister had intercepted his snow-bunny wife's path and proceeded to beat her repeatedly with a ski pole. My sister was bruised and terrified, but fortunately, no bones were broken. It created quite a stir under the pines of Sugarbush. My brother set out like a hired assassin to find the offender, flying over moguls and swishing around trees, only to witness the abuser screeching out of the lodge parking in his Mercedes. The next year my brother's friend broke his leg doing a flying eagle (stoned) over a jump. I was delighted to stay cooped up with Caleb at the lodge and play checkers. He was very cute—long hair, brown eyes, James Taylor during the *Sweet Baby James* era—and I got to eat chili and stare at his face instead of becoming an ice sculpture of a despondent child.

Ultimately ski school paid off; as a teenager I was skilled enough to bomb down the mountain, and as an adult adept enough to ski the double diamonds and get whistled at by University of Arizona guys on the chairlift.

A year ago I found myself on the parent side of the ski school battle. I stuffed my children into snowsuits and sent them, weeping, to ski school as I skulked around the lodge in fur boots, with hot cocoa and my iPad. What? I gave them gum!

———— ⌘ ————

When I was thirteen, we spent Christmas break in Cuernavaca, Mexico. My brother was nineteen, my sister eighteen, my little sister seven. The first few days were festive, filled with guacamole, day trips to ancient Mexican temples, and the purchasing of many colorful embroidered Mexican blouses. And then, all at once, we were struck down with Montezuma's revenge—a condition that had us fighting for the bathroom as our intestines rebelled more forcefully than the Mexican Revolution.

My mother decided to kill four birds with one

stone. She lined us up facedown on her bed with our pants down at our ankles. One by one, she inserted a glycerin suppository up our bums like she was putting nickels in a slot machine. I'd hear "OW, Mom!" going down the line until she got to me. I guess you could call it premeditated insurrection, but there was no getting the medicine in my fanny. You know when you touch a sea urchin, and it instantly puckers closed? My anus was Batman's car. By the fourth try the suppository had disintegrated; there were only two foil-wrapped bullets left, and one was earmarked for my little sister. My mother, in full no-antidiarrhea-capsule-will-get-the-better-of-me mode, unwrapped the capsule and pushed it in like she was Dirty Harry loading a gun.

All went smoothly with my younger sister, and then my stomach cramped. The butter bullet flew out of my body across the room and hit the middle of a painting depicting a toucan in a sombrero. I'm sure if I rehearsed it, it would have been an excellent party trick, especially in Tijuana, but shocking and extraordinary as it was, I wasn't sure how the room would react. "Well, that was your one shot, and now it's gone," said my mother. As if it were my fault I had a sassy ass. My recovery took longer than the others', but from that day on I knew I was gifted. You should see me in childbirth.

Flash forward three decades, back to the Bahamas. By the end of the week and a bottle of (no doubt expired) antibiotic potion, my daughter had recovered. We headed to Atlantis, a place for children to shoot down urine-flooded water slides and parents to consider ending their lives. One afternoon ten buses of Herbalife employees arrived, and as I ran to avoid them, I slipped on a soggy diaper. If I hadn't had the strength, or had been ten years older, I would have been trampled by the hordes of people gearing up for their third crème brulée frappuccino before hitting the slide again. My husband continued being smacked by the sides of the ginormous Aztec pyramid slide, occasionally surfacing like a wet monkey. I spent the time out front searching for a vacant taxi.

The next morning we were back in New York. I lay in my bed, it was sleeting outside, and I watched *The View* while surfing eBay on my iPad. My husband was at work, my kids were at school, and the dogs had finally peed directly on the wee wee pad. Finally, vacation.

CHAPTER TWENTY-FOUR

ali sells seashells

I have an obsession with seashells. No, not like people who have a chunk of coral in their bookcase or an abalone ashtray they picked up in Tortola. I dream about them, I travel for them, I surf the Internet for them, I stalk them.

Twelve years ago I went to Anguilla. I was snorkeling—always no deeper than four feet, because a great white could at minimum take an arm. I spotted a small pink knuckle protruding from the white sand and dove down to explore it. I pulled and jimmied until I yanked to the surface a stunning bullmouth helmet shell. To many people this shell may look like a large pair of pink Botoxed lips, but to me it was one of the most beautiful things I had ever seen. The fact that a gorgeous specimen like that was created by nature and nestled in the sea was mind-blowing. And, it was free! My heart was racing; it was like finding a briefcase of cash in an Amtrak station or a mismarked dress in the sale bin. From that day on, diving for shells became a metaphor for my life—the idea of putting myself out there in an undefined and unpredictable world, pursuing a goal fraught with danger (barracudas, sharks, producers) and achieving it. And the achievement comes with a tangible reward, a natural piece of art or an Emmy. So it became imperative to travel to some location with seashells at least once a year. Because I wasn't winning any Emmys.

I tried to downplay the whole seashell insanity before George and I were hitched. When I was on my honeymoon, I casually pulled out my snorkel and "went for a quick dip" while he sat on the beach and read his fourth novel of the day. I was literally swept away. I thought I had been diving for twenty minutes; I was in the water for four hours. It must be what porn addicts experience—they think they've been cruising the Web for a few minutes, and yet they've grown a full beard and the dog is emaciated. It led to the only tiff on what was otherwise a sublime vacation. I returned home with two hotel duffels full of limpets, moon shells, turbans, whelks, and babylons. I should add that when I was living alone in Los Angeles, I bought an eight-foot French display case to house my treasures, along with two bookcases. The expense of moving across country was not the abundance of flea market furniture, but the thousands of shells that needed to be individually wrapped in bubble wrap like they were live kidneys.

When we had our second child, our house was ripping at the seams. The tiny guest room became the baby room, and the broom closet became the playroom, and our bed became the kitchen, and so on. We bought a spacious Georgian-style house in Georgetown, with enough of a terrace to house dog shit for the duration of winter. The only downside of the buy was that it put me back to a house similar to the one I was raised in. I couldn't scrape the walls fast enough; I spent the next few months with night sweats trying to decide between buttercup or lemon custard paint swatches (why did we ever go off the simple primary colors)? It was enough that I was back in the city where I was raised, in a house similar to the one I escaped. I had to create an environment that said, "Yes, I am Muffie's daughter and George's wife, but I am different! I have spirit, yes I do, I have spirit—how 'bout you?" I wanted bold colors and animal prints, reflective of my chutzpah.

The trick was, what carpeting goes with that sensibility? When you walked in the front door of our house, the first thing you saw was an eye-popping pink silk sofa beneath a Lucian Freud sketch of a naked, depressed, reclining woman. That was a good start. The first time my mother entered, she paused. "THAT'S the first thing you want people to see when they walk in?" To which I casually answered, "Tits? Yup." My husband labeled the living room the shell room. Painted a soothing lavender-greyhound gray, it was intended to be a reflective, serene oasis, but in reality it could have passed for the rec room in the Museum of Natural History.

George finally put a moratorium on my shell hoarding: I could bring back no more than four per trip. And no more shells in the bed. So began a new obsession: collecting shell tchotchkes—everything from porcelain bowls in the shape of shells, pewter shell bookends, shell mirrors, shell prints and a few giant clam shells for the fireplaces . . . Yes, the first step to a cure is admitting you have a problem.

People get excited over many things. I've seen men reduced to their primal, simian selves over a Mets game, women stampeding gates at a Milly's sample sale, and preteen girls screaming outside the Trump Hotel to get a peek at a Jonas brother. This is me at the annual Brimfield flea market. And to go with a purpose—storage facilities to fill. The summer I went after we bought the house, I had to rent the largest U-Haul the company allows an unlicensed trucker. You have not lived until you're parking your vehicle in a meadow outside ten football fields of antique clutter and loot after a lunch of Friendly's fried clams and French fries. Frost, Shaw, Emerson, Gibran—not one of them could articulate the euphoria; maybe the guy who saw the Virgin Mary's face in his cereal. In my ecstatic frenzy of consumption I was able to fill the truck with a limestone kitchen island, a textile mill table, paintings of naked women, industrial lights, wicker chairs and . . . shells on Lucite stands.

What's that? Shells in western Massachusetts? In the middle of an uncut field, hidden among the antique stands and lobster roll and lemonade tents, was a truck. At first I feared it was a mirage: shells right smack in the middle of a meadow? This truck was filled with shells, coral, coral lamps, shell stone garden decorations, iron shell gates, and even authentic lavender sea fans. I dropped to my knees. The cherry on top was the owner of the haul. He was a very tan man in his early thirties with bright white teeth and chin-length ebony hair. He looked like a Native American model in a Ralph Lauren ad, complete with tastefully tattered jeans. I don't want to sound superficial—he was an attractive man in that *Dances with Wolves*, make-love-in-a-sweat-lodge-on-animal-skins-and-never-commit kind of way—but honestly, it was more about his booty. Not his backside booty, but his marine life booty.

Hundreds of dollars later, Daniel Day-Lewis completed the Herculean task of reconfiguring the contents of my overstuffed van—a task that necessitated yanking off his T-shirt (from the back to the front, hunk-style) and collecting his hair in a ponytail. I all but pulled out my Buddy Holly glasses, tapped a cigar, and told him I could make him a star! Instead, he gave me his business card; he owns a shop in Austin where he creates all his aquatic housewares. As I drove away, I watched him pull out a cigarette in my rearview mirror. If it didn't cause cancer, it would be so sexy . . .

So the aforementioned living room that was made for brass carriage light fixtures and foxhunting prints was transformed into what looked like a whaling museum in Rhode Island. But for the rug. I had bought a twenty-foot white wool sisal carpet that covered the entire floor. It brought out the luminescence of the shells' interior cavities. I know, something we all look for. But this was not the best choice for a family with children, a Norfolk puppy, and an ancient, incontinent dachshund. It was soon splattered with urine and smelled like a Porta-Potti at a truck stop in Death Valley. I begged my husband for a new rug, only to be continually rebuffed with, "Honey, it's a recession! We are not buying a new living room rug for the dogs to pee on!" So I bought some purple RIT dye and a pair of rubber gloves from the local Safeway. And with a plastic cup, and the fortitude of De Kooning, I swirled the dye in frenetic strokes over every inch of the rug, which, inadvertently, created starfishlike designs. When George returned home that night, he fumed, "I told you we cannot get a rug right now!" To which (and this is very rare in marriage) I got to dance around explaining while simultaneously flicking him the finger.

The only room beside my shell sanctuary that mattered to me was my girls' room. I thought it was essential they share a room and learn to cohabitate, be considerate of others, share their things . . . and I wanted an office. My children are extroverts, full of whimsy and slaves to Disney fashion. They requested peace-sign wallpaper and Hannah Montana quilts, which, I promised them, would come to pass when they were older (and I was dead). Instead, I painted their room a raspberry pink and installed wall-to-wall zebra carpeting. The mirrors and trim were a high-gloss white, and the curtains a subtle red and pink zigzag pattern. I hand-painted Regency chairs and re-upholstered them in deep pink velvet. It was old Hollywood glamour with a sense of humor, girly without unicorns and fairies. When they walked in for the first time they threw their arms up and screamed like the women who get called on *The Price Is Right*.

I had finally created an ecosystem that pleased everyone. There were some rooms that were soothing variations of manly brown, with thousands of books and an uncomplicated TV system for my husband; a delightful and enviable room for my girls; and my shell shack. Interestingly enough, I found out years later that my grandmother had been an avid collector and had donated her collection to Harvard University. So addiction is clearly hereditary and not learned.

A few months after settling in, Elliott (who was then five years old) was experiencing nightmares and took to crawling into our bed every night around midnight. It was classic behavior for children her age. They discover that the world is not as safe as they thought, and that evil exists; the nasty queen or mean stepmother in the fairy tales starts to press on their subconscious, and they begin to experience fear and understand that life encompasses danger. Elliott would cuddle next to me, and I would explain that it was only a dream and monsters don't exist. (Which was difficult because she watched *World News*.)

I was attempting to hose the dog poop off our terrace one afternoon in early April. It was getting warm out, and we wanted to eat dinner outside. I was wistfully watching the excrement stream across the slate tiles down the back steps and settle next to our neighbors' garage. The phone rang, so I left the hose to flood a few hibiscus plants. It was my mother. I told her I was composting.

We discussed, as we do most days, what all my siblings were up to, how the weather was in the town she was calling from, and how horribly the government was dealing with the economy and how I should hide my money under the bed. I filled her in on the headlines of our life. And then I decided to tell her about Elliott's nightmares. "It's normal for a child her age; they are realizing that the world is not safe, and . . ." I went on about the psychological ramifications of dreams and nightmares. I paused, waiting for her take—maybe I

had had nightmares? How did she cope with her children and sleepless nights?

There was a long pause. "Well," she began, "did
you ever think it might have something to do with
how you decorated her room?"

CHAPTER TWENTY-FIVE

i was born this way

My grandmother constructed a raft out of seventy-six yak hides upon which she sailed down the Yellow River in Lanzhou, China. Yes. True story. My mother's mother. There is a female gene in our family that is so dominant it devours, like a wild boar, any weak link that dares cross its path. And the result is a long line of women whose skin may be pallid and pasty, but it's tough.

My grandmother trekked across the Mongolian desert for three years on camelback exploring subcultures and discovering lost kingdoms. She was born a quiet debutante from Boston with no real future plans, except maybe to one day needlepoint a hymn. She was forbidden to attend Bryn Mawr as the narrow-minded and strict patriarch of the family believed that "ladies do not go to college." She could have spent her life setting her hair in pincurls for Junior League lunches or bleaching her white gloves, but instead chose to join the Red Cross and sail to France. She eventually married an anthropologist/scientist, a real loner. I'm not sure I could hunker down with a man who prefers entomology to . . . well, anything. His job took her to China, far from the comforts of Boston. The lace Victorian dresses were replaced by a leather coat, pilot sunglasses, and lace-up military boots. She was the original Lara Croft, Tomb Raider. My grandmother would march ten hours in rough winds in the Alashan desert and still photograph Mongols and aid birthing camels while deciding what herbivore concoction to prepare at the campsite.

My mother raised four children while reigning as one of the most successful and feared women in D.C. She, too, was a debutante from Boston and a self-described wallflower. But when that gene kicked in, *Kapow!* She founded corporations, sat on boards instrumental in changing the country's arts and culture, and worked for a president. By the way, she just called me from a barge in a country whose name I can't pronounce.

My mom, after planting thirty peony bushes, was weeding her vegetable garden in Virginia one summer afternoon. My mother can seed a lettuce patch as seamlessly as she can welcome Mao-Tse Tung in Mandarin. I had come down for the weekend to escape my first-floor Manhattan studio apartment with bars on the one window that faced the Dumpsters. I plopped down on the grass dangerously close to some dog poop and watched her toil. We sat in complete silence, save for the yelps of a foxhound that lived next door and always sounded like his paw was stuck in a meat grinder.

"I think I should move to L.A.," I blurted out. She kept weeding. "I just think as an actress I should be where the work is?" The gene was kicking in. Okay, I wasn't contemplating fighting Ukrainian civil disobedience or saving the rain forest, but Los Angeles is rough (especially if you don't have a gym membership).

My mother put down her soft-grip pruner and trowel. "I'm not going to tell you what you should or should not do," she said. How is that ever a good answer? But, she continued, "You have to follow your gut. If you truly believe that is what you need to do, then you should listen and do it."

This left me with two conflicting scenarios. I could stand up abruptly, kicking dirt and yell, "Screw you, you just want me to go to L.A. for your own selfishness! Well, I'm not! I'm staying right here and working at the Olive Garden. Nice try, MOTHER!" Aside from this being nonsensical and psychotic, it didn't seem like the right moment for rebellion. Instead, I opted for her support and wisdom. I left for Los Angeles a month later, a city where I had never been and where I didn't know a soul.

My grandmother schlepped to China carrying eleven pieces of luggage and guns, in anticipation of Shanghai's civil unrest. Starvation had plagued the countryside to the point that peasants flung themselves upon the train tracks my grandmother rode on. My mother moved to Washington, D.C., in the nineteen sixties, during the country's fight for civil rights. She was with Bobby Kennedy, for whom she campaigned, when he was shot. Months after moving to Hollywood, I experienced the Los Angeles riots. I sat on my friend's apartment roof eating dry cereal and watched the smoke and chaos exploding in front of me. A weaker person would have called United Airlines and gotten the hell out of there! Well, I did call United, but the riots were smack in the middle between the airport and me, so I couldn't move. The point is, I fearlessly pursued my passion anyway.

My older sister, Sissy, gave birth three times without any drugs and my younger sister, Fiona, can psychologically disrobe anyone—whether they be Jungian or Freudian. And me? I've jumped out of a plane, been on live TV without any self-editing mechanisms, and can bake a mean cupcake. My own daughters can bloody a nurse's nose at the mere mention of a flu shot and aren't deterred by the word "no." Ever. My eldest can scream so shockingly loud that in these moments she should be on the back of a Siberian tiger waving an axe and shield, leading her tribe into battle, not being told she can't stay up and watch *Modern Family*. Someday, however, that inner fire will serve her well. Preferably after she's left home.

And so I know that my own daughters, with this mighty gene, if channeled correctly have the capacity to conquer the world. I'm not pressuring them to do that; inventing an anti-wrinkle cream that actually works would make me just as proud.

CHAPTER TWENTY-SIX

the eyes have it

I am not a vain person. In fact, I should care more. I bite my nails till they bleed, don't work out, and wait until my dark roots are so grown out I look like one of those women who holds her Big Gulp in her cleavage and mails her panties to convicts. I'm in awe of my girlfriends with resplendent bodies perfectly toned from Pilates, skin that has been thermo- or phyto- or *something*-dermed, and silky hair from exotic oils drawn from rare coconut husks. If I shower, shave my pits, and moisturize? I consider it a full day of pampering.

So the idea of plastic surgery seemed inane and way too time-consuming. Who would elect to have someone cut his or her face? What woman could suffer through a face-lift? Seep her stitched and tattered flesh in a bucket of ice for weeks in a dark, undisclosed hotel room? Surely, I thought in my ignorance, only Joan Rivers and a handful of the women who elbow me out of the way at the Bergdorf's sale had "work" done. Little did I know that a significant por-tion of my friends were nipping and tucking, slicing and dicing on a daily basis.

My friend Beezie is ravishing. Her eyes are symmetrically perfect, her skin creamy and seemingly untouched by the sun (although I once saw a freckle on her ear), her legs toned from years of tennis. In other words, even as a middle-aged mother of four, she can still wear tiny jean shorts and look like Cheryl Ladd circa 1976. Beezie is a professional photographer. Her pictures are as crisp and clear as she is. And when she's staring at me midconversation, I can't help but feel she's deciding how to "fix me in post." Ah, to be airbrushed through life . . .

Beezie was in New York for a few days, and we met at the downtown eatery Lucky Strike for french fries and the hope of recapturing our youth. My costume for such a performance included skinny jeans and high-top sneakers, not that I was fooling anyone. I could have been our waiter's great-grandmother. I remember once being at a bar in Beverly Hills and seeing a gaggle of girls in microskirts and stilettoed, bejeweled cowboy boots sipping pomegranate martinis, laughing and barking like baby seals while whipping their bleached hair from side to side. When they finally got up to leave and turned around, to my horror I saw that they were not a day younger than sixty-seven. Since then I've been pushing myself to dress age appropriately. And I don't judge a woman's age from her behind even if she's in diapers.

Beezie looked especially becoming this spring day. Like she had just emerged from six months in a hyperbaric chamber.

"I got my eyes done!" she declared as she batted her lids up and down.

"I don't know what that means?" I inquired, shoving a bunch of ketchup-drenched fries down my gullet.

"I got all that hanging skin on my upper lids cut off," she answered.

Instantly I was aware of the skin above my brows enveloping my eyes like a down comforter.

It's important to note at this point (as I was frequently reminded by haters on the comment pages of the Internet) that I had quite large bags under my eyes. And it's not because I was up all night doing speed balls or studying for the bar exam. It's a hereditary condition passed down from generation to generation, like chipped china or a propensity to drink. My baggy eyes had been a source of utter frustration not only to my reflection but also to makeup artists (who whispered sotto voce about them on set) and cinematographers (who spent hours desperately trying to relight my face). And if I had too much salt or soy sauce? I awoke the next morning as Mickey Rourke. I tried every concealer, Preparation H, and even Scotch tape, but there my dark and aging baggage hung on skin (that was already losing elasticity), like pizza dough thrown against the wall.

I wanted Beezie's bright and awake eyes. I wanted her body, too, but baby steps. One would involve being drugged to a twilight state; the other, thousands of SoulCycle spin classes.

I consulted every expert professional ravisher I knew, including four beauty editors and a bevy of gay men. I was referred to three doctors. I chose the female doctor based solely on the fact that I assumed she would be nicer when I yanked off my shower cap and went screaming into plate glass en route from the operating table. And I hoped she throw in a free Pap smear.

The office of Dr. Saleh (not her real name) was pristine. It was so immaculate and speckless they could have performed open-heart surgery on me on the bathroom floor.

Dr. Saleh herself was statuesque and flawless. I pointed to her face and (like a toddler) drooled, "I want that! I want that!"

She inspected my face like a gemologist scrutinizing a blood diamond. "You have heavy bags. It's very advanced for a woman your age. I highly recommend you get this procedure as soon as you can. You also have sagging around your neck and—"

I cut her off. I didn't want her distracted by lopsided breasts and ears in desperate need of pinning. I took her first available surgical opening.

As I confided in friends and family about the upcoming procedure, I was stunned to learn that my weary-looking eyes had been the bane of other people's existences as well. The news was met with the same unanimous response: "You must be so excited. . . . Finally! We've been collecting donations for this for years! There's enough for boobs, too!"

The more people I opened up to about my plans, the more people confessed to having gone under the knife themselves. The word "blepharoplasty" was whispered like "abortion" was in the 1950s. Over 50 percent of the women I spoke to admitted to having had their eyes tweaked. And it didn't stop there. Everything from the forehead to the vagina (vaginoplasty deserves its own chapter), down to the knees. Byron coined the phrase "the fatal gift of beauty." Now, if you're not born with it, you can buy it!

On the big day I arrived at a Parisian-looking townhouse at the crack of dawn. There was a discreet side entrance for people like Madonna, some kind of Underground Railroad for the immortal celebrity, but I marched in the front door wearing a name tag and blaring a bullhorn. I was in complete denial about the fact that I was volunteering (at a hefty cost) to have my face slashed.

The anesthesiologist was a strapping man in his thirties with perfect teeth and a sun-kissed look that suggested a second home. He was so charming that I felt entirely comfortable allowing him to pierce my wrist with an IV as he regaled me with stories about his new Mercedes SL550. He explained he was going to administer a cocktail in my arm that would make me very relaxed, like I had had a couple glasses of wine. The syringe went into my IV line and I fell into the deepest level of sleep. A couple glasses of wine? More like a couple gallons of chloroform.

I remember being held up like a drunken sorority girl as a (far too attractive) nurse and my husband pulled me across the marble floor of our lobby. I was told my first question when I awoke after surgery was "Did they shave my pubic hair?" Apparently anesthesia makes me feisty because I also tried to yank off my husband's trousers in the elevator.

In the days that followed I lay in my bed with blurry vision and ice packs on my eyes and listened to reruns of *Friends* on TV. (The show still stands up even without visuals. And in Spanish.) Every few hours the nurse handed me fistfuls of pills, including Vicodin. For a lightweight like me, one Vicodin is not unlike a puppy chewing a sheet of acid. It alleviated the pain but rendered my limbs numb, and for a few hours I believed I was Eva Longoria.

I decided openness about the procedure was the best route to take with my kids. I explained that I had looked like I was sleep-deprived for the past twenty years and I was tired of looking tired. It was my Moby-Dick. Whether or not they fully grasped what I was telling them, I felt good about being honest. Even though they were confused that I chose to fix my eyes when to them, my stomach was clearly the glaring problem.

———— ⌘ ————

My mother thinks plastic surgery is "for the birds." Maybe, if they have a deviated septum in their beaks. But she did have the same operation—upper blepharoplasty. I called her a few days before my appointment and told her I was going under the knife on my quest for shaving (or cutting) years off my face. Her voice had that disparaging yet concerned tone only she can manage: "Well, I hope you have a good doctor."

I decided to pull the gauze off the conversation. "Well, Mom, don't forget that *you* had this surgery!"

There was a long pause, long enough to allow a Manhattan bus to power by.

"Well." If such a thing is possible, her tone had grown even firmer. "That's because I lost my peripheral vision."

Right. So, from now on, let's say I was legally blind. And now I see!

I think I do look less haggard now. But we live in a world of never enough. When I emailed a photo of myself to one of my beauty magazine pals, he screeched with excitement, "Amazing! Don't you love them? Now, just a little Restylane around the mouth, some Botox and a neck lift, and you're good to go!"

acknowledgments

To Kathy Schneider for starting the ball rolling; my exceptional editor, Jennifer Barth; Lydia Weaver; Beth Silfin; Archie Ferguson; Leah Wasielewski; Leslie Cohen; Tina Andreadis; Jason Sack; and everyone at HarperCollins.

For my agents extraordinaire, Rhonda Price and Phyllis Wender, and my lawyer, Adam Kaller, who is so dedicated even though I made him two dollars last year.

To Richard and Mona; Melanie; Peter; Holly; Brother Tom; and Paulina—for all your insights and support.

Michael and James for everything, including the lavish book party I'm going to ask them to throw.

To Joel and Ebs who dealt with my persistent asks and delivered like gods.

To Jessica, for all her love and always getting the joke. And Jerry, who makes ME feel funny.

Michelle, my sister, who always has my back.

To Oprah, thank you—wish I had finished this last year!

And to all my Lady Loves—Mariska; Christa; Katie; Sarah C.; Napsy; and all my Baby Love girls— it's our friendship that fuels me.

To my family—this book could not have been written without our craziness.

And love. John, Sissy, and Fiona—in a broken nest there are always a few whole eggs.

And to my husband, George, always my best adviser, love of my life, and (secretly) a fellow comedian.

about the author

Ali Wentworth made a name for herself on the comedy show *In Living Color*, and has made appearances on such television shows as *The Tonight Show with Jay Leno*; *Seinfeld* (playing Schmoopie in the "Soup Nazi" episode); *Head Case* (which she created, wrote, and executive produced); and *The Oprah Winfrey Show*, for which she was a correspondent. Her movie credits include *Jerry Maguire*, *The Real Blonde*, *Office Space*, and *The Love Bug*; most recently, she appeared in *It's Complicated* with Meryl Streep, Steve Martin, and Alec Baldwin.

A native of Washington, D.C., Wentworth lives in New York City with her husband, George Stephanopoulos, their two girls, and two unhousebroken dachsunds.